Leadership

Faults & Fixes

*Pressing the Refresh Button in
Business, Government
and Society*

JOHN MITCHELL

ISBN-13: 978-1535230667
ISBN-10: 1535230665

Published by Mitchell Leadership Consulting Ltd.
www.mitchell-lc.com   contact@mitchell-lc.com

Testimonials

Microsoft UK: David Svendsen, former CEO

"I shall be forever grateful for the contribution John Mitchell made to my organization... in the period John worked with me, the business grew from 40 people and revenue of 15 million dollars to 900 people and over a billion dollars. That wasn't easy: it was fast growth and John's programs were fundamental in achieving direction that the company needed.

"The R&D that underpins these programs – well, they are unique and ideal for any leader who wishes for the business to expand, to grow, and to be a long-term asset."

ABN AMRO Private Banking: Reinout van Lennep, former Head of International Private Banking

"John Mitchell is a professional in every sense of the word... long track record, very international... technically and theoretically very well grounded, and when it comes to leadership issues he is particularly knowledgeable... a good listener and a good speaker, in that order... firm and outspoken, be it in a respectful and tactful way... people immediately feel comfortable with him... empathy, multi-jurisdictional and -cultural experience, language skills – in my view, John has them all."

(For complete texts, see http://mitchell-lc.com)

Allen & Overy (Global Full-Service Law Firm): Martin Pexton, Former Global HR Director

"Mitchell Leadership Consulting partnered Allen & Overy to help build sustainable global expansion, a 'one-firm' ethos and professional leadership capabilities to ensure that that the different disciplines and offices worked together seamlessly for clients. They met our need for a well-resourced development organization, with clarity of thought on how strategy, values and culture fit together.

"We began work with the Senior and Managing Partners, followed by a leadership development program for the most senior partners in the worldwide firm... While leadership remained a key theme, there was also a strong business development component.

"The programme had a significant beneficial impact on the cultural and strategic development of the firm, and helped to increase the level of professionalism in the so called soft disciplines to complement the technical expertise of the firm.

"Successful professionals tend to be demanding and critical, and are quick to spot weakness in any argument. To work effectively, programmes require high levels of intellectual credibility and well-developed cultural sensitivity... Mitchell Leadership Consulting has proven expertise in these areas."

Contents

Preface

This book is written to fill a void.

There is no reference work that gives an underlying philosophy, practical guide or "grammar" of leadership or that connects psychological and organizational aspects with business, government and society.

Leadership Faults & Fixes addresses this by revealing a unique, integrated framework that identifies and links different *levels of awareness and action* with the full *spectrum of leadership contexts* from intellectual, emotional and physical intelligence to teams, departments, businesses, sovereign states and international bodies.

The book identifies three fundamental *constructive* and three fundamental *destructive* levels of quality that apply in all leadership contexts. Through this joined-up framework a new model emerges using *emotional intelligence* to assess leadership quality and potential.

Formulated as a series of 70 dualities and dichotomies around leadership themes, it aims in each case to pierce *between* the two sides of the coin and so to reveal, gradually, the coin itself – coming to a new vision of power and responsibility and of what connects them.

Acknowledgements

I wish to acknowledge three extraordinary people who have been constructive influences in my life.

 **H.E. Ardeshir Zahedi**, Foreign Minister and Ambassador of Iran in Washington and London during the time of his friend and father-in-law the Shah, has given me unique perspectives and precious insights on world affairs over countless dinners since we first met as neighbours in Montreux in 2004.

A central political figure through the 1960's and 1970's, he knew and was friendly with most if not all heads of state during that period and has maintained many high level contacts and friendships through the nearly 40 years since the revolution. I am especially grateful to him for his generosity in opening doors for me to meet with and listen to a wide variety of public figures in the US, Europe and Middle East and so to explore many questions that have interested me concerning government and politics.

Of his many unusual talents and gifts, the one that I have found most admirable and instructive is his ability to maintain warm and valued friendships with people of all types and backgrounds, irrespective of their opinions.

 Moving from the outer to the inner world, I'm truly fortunate to have enjoyed regular contact with **Dr. Michel de Salzmann** in Paris, Geneva and elsewhere during his latter years. Quiet, and with a profound understanding of the human condition, he nourished both my research in contemplative disciplines and my efforts to think freely and inclusively.

 Bridging the outer and inner worlds is "performance," and in this context I'm privileged to have been connected to the great English pianist **Mr. John Vallier**, joining with his family members during the 1970's and 1980's to promote his return to the concert platform after a long absence. Throughout demanding tours including sell-out concerts at Carnegie Hall, New York and the Royal Festival Hall, London, he exemplified humility, authenticity and rigorous preparation in weaving a magical effect on audiences and critics.

This book is dedicated to these three very different men, each masterly in their field and each sensing that "things will get worse before they get better" while retaining an unshakeable conviction of a positive future for humanity.

John Mitchell
Montreux, Switzerland
July 2016

Overview of Faults and Fixes

Each "Fault" presents a *duality* reflecting a Level +1 mindset. Each "Fix" lifts this towards Level +2 or +3, and some offer practical suggestions. The meaning of these "Levels" is explained in the first few pages.

FAULTS (Level +1 Thinking)	FIXES (+2 and +3 Thinking)
Mindset	
1. Leader or Manager?	1. Visualize *Authority!*
2. Good or Bad?	2. See *Levels* of Mindset!
3. Leader or Follower?	3. Visualize *Responsibility!*
4. Nature or Nurture?	4. Expand your *Questioning!*
5. Level +3 or not?	5. Recognize *Aspirations!*
6. Bored or Stressed?	6. Set *New Direction!*
7. Too Busy or Tired?	7. Say *"No"* to Passivity!
8. Change or Growth?	8. Raise *Leadership Mindset!*
9. Agree or Disagree?	9. Study *Reactions!*
10. Courses or Books?	10. Conduct *Live* Research!
Three Types of Intelligence	
11. Intelligent or Unintelligent?	11. See *Levels* of Intelligence!
12. Like or Dislike?	12. Create *Intent!*
13. Yes or No?	13. Translate Intent *into Metrics!*
14. Tense or Relaxed?	14. Get *Grounded!*
15. Love or Hate?	15. Get Free from *Inner Conditions!*
16. Right or Wrong?	16. Develop *Threefoldness!*
17. Good or Bad Appetites?	17. Generate *Vitality!*
18. Free Will or Fate?	18. *Observe* the Filter!
19. Yes... BUT!	19. Use Personality as *Food!*
20. Heaven or Hell?	20. Acknowledge *Commonality!*

Leadership Faults & Fixes

FAULTS (Level +1 Thinking)	FIXES (+2 and +3 Thinking)
Communicating as a Leader	
21. Hire or Reject?	21. Define Roles *Creatively!*
22. Delegate or Hoard?	22. *Empower!*
23. Review or Not?	23. Connect *Needs* to *Aspirations!*
24. Confront or Avoid?	24. Create *Inner* Confrontation!
25. Complain or Leave It?	25. Recommend *Improvements!*
26. Difficult Clients or Colleagues?	26. Align to Others' *Filters!*
27. Meeting or Preaching?	27. *Raise* Mindset Levels!
28. Creative or Stuck?	28. *Pre*-Brainstorm!
29. Win or Lose?	29. Create *Joint Contribution!*
30. Dysfunctional Team or Group?	30. Help the Team *Visualize* Itself!
Organizations and Departments	
31. Order or Chaos?	31. See *Organizational* Quality!
32. Hierarchical or Flat?	32. See Organizational *Responsibility!*
33. Strategy or No Strategy?	33. *Be Strategic!*
34. Values and Competencies?	34. Build Quality into *Planning!*
35. Departments or Compartments?	35. Plan Using *360 Thinking!*
36. Local or Global?	36. *Cascade* 360 Planning!
37. Can't attract or retain?	37. Manage *"Dead Wood"!*
38. Initiatives or Consultants?	38. *Coaching and Mentoring!*
39. Accountable or Unaccountable?	39. Develop a *Culture of Coaching!*
40. Top-Down or Bottom-Up?	40. Reciprocal *Nourishment!*

Overview of Faults and Fixes (contd.)

FAULTS (Level +1 Thinking)	FIXES (+2 and +3 Thinking)
Government, Citizens and Education	
41. Information or Knowledge?	41. Build *Understanding!*
42. Democracy or Tyranny?	42. Recognize *Oligarchies!*
43. Sovereignty or Federalism?	43. *Subsidiarity!*
44. Constitution or Not?	44. See the *Role* of Government!
45. Manifesto or Plan	45. Make Policies *Strategic!*
46. Right or Left?	46. *Multi-Party* Representation!
47. PR or FPTP?	47. Put *Tactics* into Context!
48. Race or Gender?	48. *Constructive Inclusion!*
49. Big Business & Big Government?	49. *Threefold* Social Structure!
50. Schools or Academies?	50. Think *Higher!*
Measuring and Transforming Leadership	
51. Extravert or Introvert?	51. Measure *Mindset!*
52. 360 or Engagement Surveys?	52. Measure *Communication!*
53. Coercive or Affiliative?	53. Measure *Responsibility!*
54. Off-sites or Jollies?	54. Measure *Teams & Organization!*
55. Giver or Receiver?	55. Measure *your Citizenship!*
56. Vote or Not Bother?	56. Measure *your Government!*
57. Fragmented Measurement?	57. *Joined-Up* Measurement!
58. Assessment or Development?	58. Plan for *Transformation!*
59. Tomorrow or Next Month?	59. *Coaching – Now!*
60. Coaching or Self-Coaching?	60. *Transcend Duality!*

Leadership Faults & Fixes

FAULTS (Level +1 Thinking)	FIXES (+2 and +3 Thinking)
The Future of Leadership, Culture and Humanity	
61. Progress or Regress?	61. See *Repetition!*
62. War or Peace?	62. See, Feel and Admit *Error!*
63. Debt and Credit?	63. Review the *Purpose* of Money!
64. Cancer and Terrorism	64. *Transparency!*
65. Dependence or Independence?	65. *Inter-Dependence!*
66. Science or Religion?	66. Recognize *Decay!*
67. Crime and Punishment!	67. Repair and *Prepare!*
68. Free Speech or "Correctness"?	68. Build *Attentiveness!*
69. Fed up with "Strategy"?	69. Think *Differently!*
70. Life or Death?	70. Press the *Refresh Button!*

Leadership Faults & Fixes

Mindset

Our mindset has a threefold structure.

It is made up of intellectual, emotional and physical intelligence. Through these emerge the ideas, attitudes and practices that enable and limit leadership thinking, communicating and consequent impact.

To the extent that mindset is shared across a group, organization, nation or race, it becomes the basis of prevailing culture. And much of its content consists of unarticulated assumptions.

In this context, a Fault is not a hard and fast mistake, but an element of mindset that has yet to be opened up and examined fully.

Faults 1-10 reveal a series of dualities that typically characterize the mindsets of leaders – experienced, new and prospective. The Fixes aim to help expand awareness through adding a *third factor* or a wider perspective.

Note: in this section and throughout the book, the abbreviation FF refers to Faults and Fixes.

Fault 1:
Leader or Manager?

This frequently referenced duality assumes *exclusivity* – the answer *must* be "one or the other" – and omits a key third element, *administrator*. In reality, the same person can be all three at once! The true difference is in *levels of awareness and constructive action*.

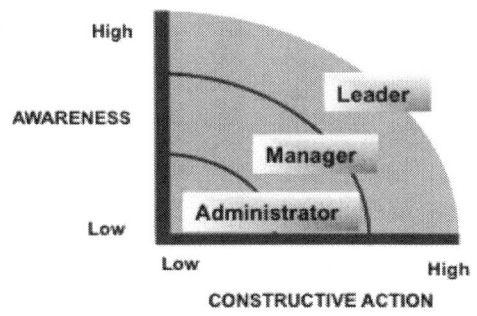

A first example of **threefoldness** and relative levels of awareness and action

Administrators execute tasks; managers control the use of resources; leaders create meaning and set direction. Management *includes and transcends* administration; leadership *includes and transcends* management.

Administration is the simplest to delegate (including to machines), followed by management. Leadership cannot be delegated (or replaced by artificial intelligence) and its quality and influence permeate the other levels.

Fix 1:
Visualize *Authority!*

Whether labeled leader, manager or administrator, you likely have *three* key types of relationship (*higher, lower* and *peer*) based on decision-making authority. With the *external* relationship, these make up your "360."

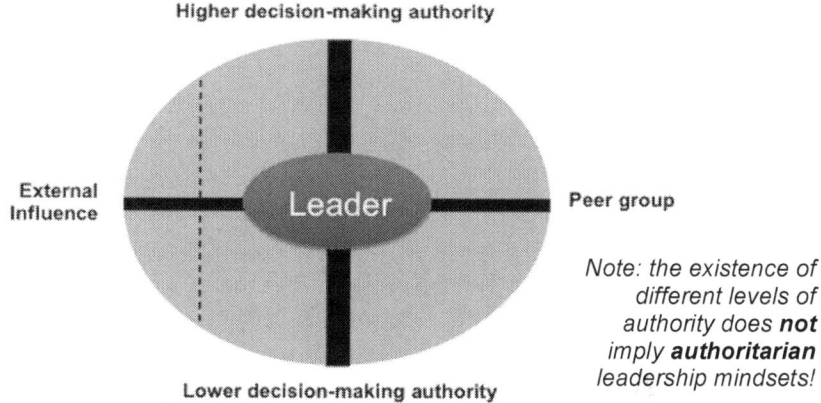

Higher decision-making authority

External Influence

Leader

Peer group

Lower decision-making authority

*Note: the existence of different levels of authority does **not** imply **authoritarian** leadership mindsets!*

This is where your leadership shows! Even if you don't have people "below" you, leadership shows in the other relationships. Its quality depends on *your mindset.*

Suggestion: draw and adapt the diagram to your own situation, showing the names of those in your personal 360 or 270. (You may find it useful to have this available while reading the coming pages.)

Fault 2:
Good or Bad?

We tend to see good and bad *subjectively* as opposites, based on what seems to benefit our "interests" (good guys with us, bad guys against, and so on).

Becoming more objective means raising awareness. The proverbial glass is neither half-full nor half-empty: it's *full* – of water and air! (a "level +3" view…)

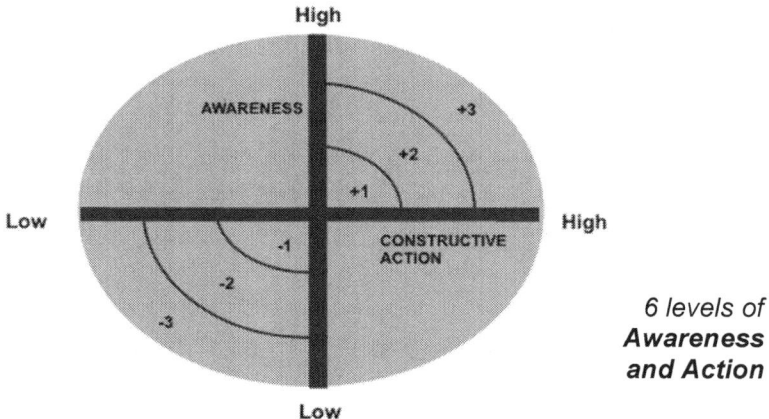

6 levels of ***Awareness and Action***

Taking the diagram from page 14 and replacing words with numbers, we can also add *negative* levels to show *6 relative levels* of awareness and constructive action. Objectively: *good* leadership *raises* awareness and constructive action; *bad* leadership does the opposite.

Fix 2:
See *Levels* of Mindset!

These 6 levels of awareness and action are verifiable through experience and provide a simple, practical tool for assessing and developing leadership mindset.

They help differentiate, for example, peacemakers and warmongers who otherwise might both be categorized as simply "leaders" without qualitative differentiation.

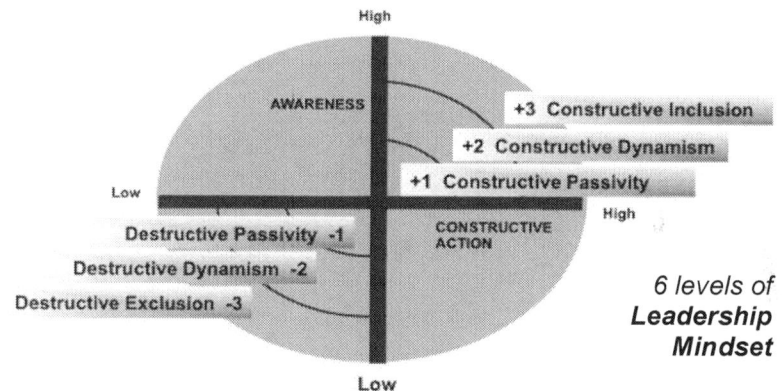

6 levels of
*Leadership
Mindset*

The 3 positive gradations are *constructive passivity, dynamism* and *inclusion;* the 3 negative gradations are *destructive passivity, dynamism* and *exclusion.* Each higher level includes and transcends the level below it, giving a picture of potential transformation.

Fault 3:
Leader or Follower?

Another misleading duality! Every leader "follows" a higher authority, whether another person or an ideology, and every leader is similarly "followed," giving the *threefold* vertical relationship shown on page 15.

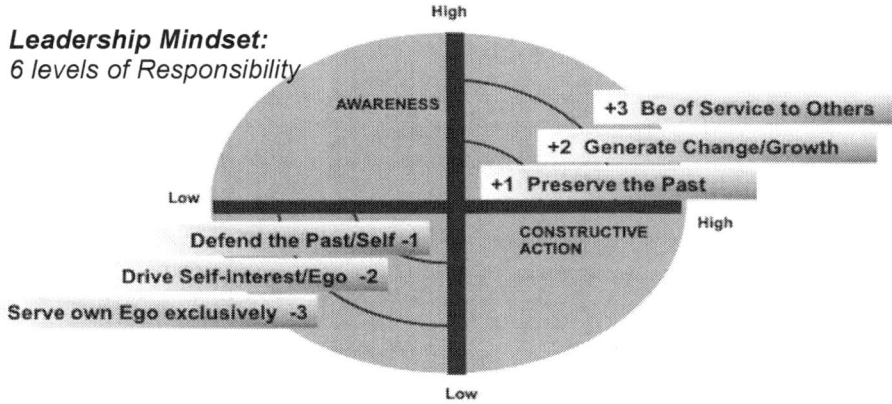

This diagram shows the sense of responsibility *felt and acted upon* at each level of leadership mindset. Again, each higher level *includes and transcends* the lower.

"Followership" often indicates a relatively passive sense of responsibility. *Suggestion:* note down *how **you** feel your leadership responsibility* in relation to your higher, lower and peer relationships.

Fix 3:
Visualize *Responsibility!*

The responsibility *felt and acted upon* at level +3 is *to be of service*. This shows in specific ways in each of the 360 relationships (see diagram below) and provides the basis for leadership direction-setting at level +3.

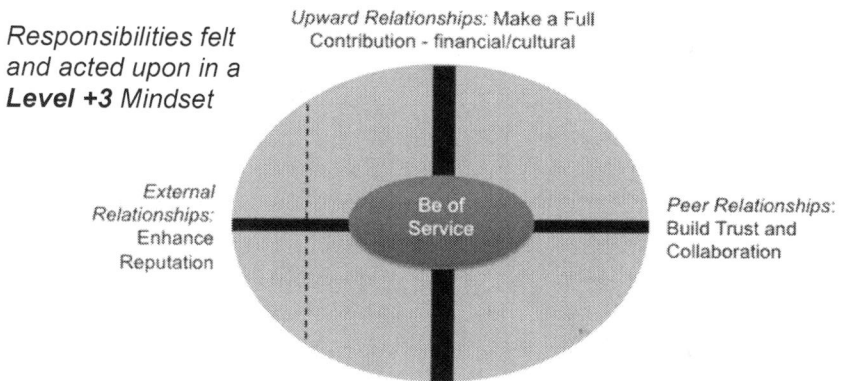

Responsibilities felt and acted upon in a **Level +3** *Mindset*

Upward Relationships: Make a Full Contribution - financial/cultural

External Relationships: Enhance Reputation

Be of Service

Peer Relationships: Build Trust and Collaboration

Downward Relationships: Create and sustain an Environment in which people contribute fully and fulfil their potential

Those in lower authority look upwards for direction and meaning. This can be exploited by a level -2 Leadership Mindset to create *subservient* "followers," or used constructively (Level +2) to help them *raise their own leadership capability.* From the viewpoint of a Level +3 Leadership Mindset, *good leadership* as defined in FF2 is needed *throughout* public and private organizations.

Fault 4:
Nature or Nurture?

A further false dichotomy, coming from +1 Mindsets, is whether or not leadership can be learned, and within that whether leaders are "born" or acquire leadership through their family or educational environment.

It's true that many people in business, government and society find themselves in leadership positions without full preparation for corresponding challenges and therefore may rely on earlier and often unconscious influences to guide them.

This can generate uncertainties, such as those implicit in Faults 1-3, often resulting in defensiveness or arrogance and generating an insecure environment for others.

Irrespective of background, the quality of leadership and the leader's ability to respond to events (literally: *responsibility*) in any case depend on *continuous learning* from real, experienced situations.

Leadership *has* to be learned, and learning can include reviewing influences from early life and their impact and legacy, so making them clearer and more conscious. *Ongoing learning*, in the form of *practical research*, is the fundamental leadership habit.

Fix 4:
Expand your *Questioning!*

The quality of leadership learning and practical research depends first on the quality of questions that we address and put to others. Again, there are 6 fundamental levels:

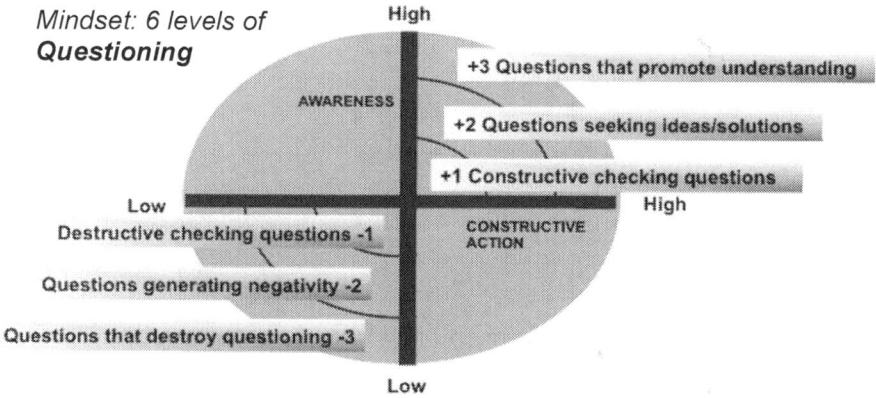

Mindset: 6 levels of **Questioning**

Suggestion: Imagine that you are leading a discussion around the subject matter of FF 1-3. Realizing that the three dualistic questions (Leader/Manager, Good/Bad, Leader/Follower) might polarize discussion and create unproductive argument, you decide to avoid using them.

What alternative questions might you raise in order to generate a more creative exchange? What will you *avoid* doing, so that the sense and reality of *research* emerges?

Fault 5:
Level +3 or not?

What was your own immediate reaction to the Levels of Mindset introduced in FF 2 and 3? Seeing this can help understand key differences between the levels.

Here are sample reactions/responses at each level:

Sample reactions/responses at each Mindset Level	
+3	"An interesting concept; I wonder how it connects to …?"
+2	"This seems new: how could it help us to achieve …?"
+1	"Am I at Level +3 or not?"
- 1	"I don't like it – it reminds me of …"
- 2	"I'm already at level +4"
- 3	"This is nonsense and doesn't concern me"

Note that the + 1, 2 and 3 responses include *questions*:
- +1 questions are typically *closed* (yes/no)
- +2 are *open* (seeking opinions, information)
- +3 are *creative* (generating new thought)

The level +1 reaction is theoretical and may indicate *aspiration*, needing help to get beyond the conceptual. Level +2 will need less help and at level +3 a connection to practice may happen unaided.

The minus levels will likely require expert influence for constructive interest to be generated.

Fix 5:
Recognize *Aspirations!*

At Level +1 there may be high awareness that is not yet connected to action and is *aspirational.* Level +1 may also feature constructive action that has been copied or learned by imitation, with the reasons or intentionality behind it not yet understood.

Note: there can be **awareness without action**, *and vice versa...*

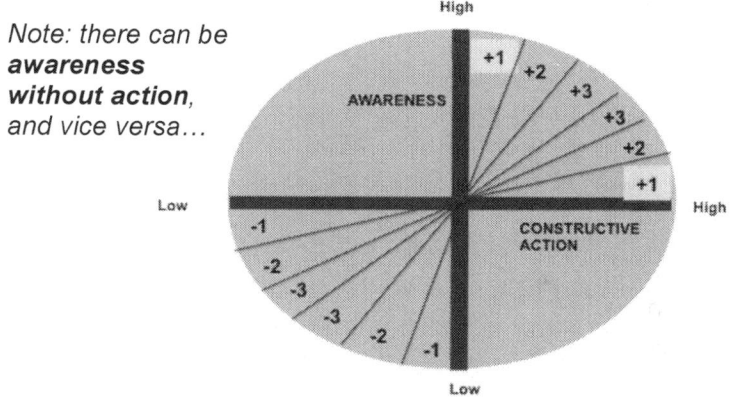

The "scissors" version (above) of the diagram from FF2 indicates this Level +1 separation between awareness and action and therefore the potential for development.

Suggestion: Note down an *aspiration* of your own – perhaps a long-standing one, or maybe one that has been generated by your reading of FF 1-4.

Fault 6:
Bored or Stressed?

Often we need to make a fresh start, and it's not clear how. Whether looking to re-energize ourselves or others, initiate a new project or email, the hardest task can be to *author* – the true meaning of *authority!*

FF 1-3 reveal the four-way relationship structure and generic responsibilities of leadership. Of these, the relationship *upwards* is the most important.

At first this may not seem to be the case, since other relationships can take much more time and effort. And leadership courses and books tend to focus almost exclusively on the *downward* relationship.

Yet *everything depends on the upward relationship!* If that relationship is lost, we most likely lose the others. It's through a strong upward relationship that leaders derive the authority to decide and act.

All leaders have an upward relationship, even if they may seem to be already at the top. For an entrepreneur starting a new business, it may be the bank manager; for a Managing Partner, the firm; for a Prime Minister, the electorate; for a Dictator, a grouping of nations.

Fix 6:
Set *New Direction!*

Making a fresh start in leadership means *renewing the upward relationship*, that is, the **contribution** to be made to the "higher authority." This is usually a person or body of people and can also be an agreement or a set of ideas or ideals that *carry authority*. Useful questions for this, whether in reflection or dialogue, can be:

1. What are the perceived needs and challenges of the "higher authority" (whether individual, Board, market, government, international assembly)?
2. What can I/we contribute in order to be of service?
3. How can this contribution be agreed and usefully measured, and over what time period?

Measures of contribution are most often *financial*, sometimes *change-related* (structural or strategic), and – rarely, yet potentially most valuably – *cultural.*

Suggestion: apply the above three questions within your own 360. Later, add in questions for the peer and downward relationships (see FF3), such as: *How can I build greater trust and collaboration? How can I improve the working environment for those I lead? How can I make the work more interesting?*

Fault 7:
Too Busy or Tired?

Even though it may only take an hour or so, Fix 6 may not happen because there's "no time" or, even if there is time, the energy for fresh thinking is not there.

We may tend to think of being busy as being *active*, because our bodies are moving or because there's plenty of online activity or personal interaction. From a level +3 point of view, being busy in this way is often a sign of *passivity*, and can lead to stress.

It's important that we enjoy leadership and that this is visible to others. Some types of enjoyment are relatively passive and transitory, stimulated by passing trends and other external factors. More active, lasting enjoyment comes from using and developing our own faculties fully and productively.

To create opportunities for this kind of enjoyment, both for ourselves and for others, we need to carve out quality preparation time and then make good use of it.

How to find the time and energy even for this setting aside of quality preparation time?!

Fix 7:
Say *"No"* to Passivity!

It may seem strange that the first step in shaping or renewing our leadership approach can be to say "No!" This doesn't necessarily mean saying the word "No!" aloud to others; it's more likely an inner "No!" to *ourselves* – to the habits and influences that tend to diminish or subvert *quality preparation time*.

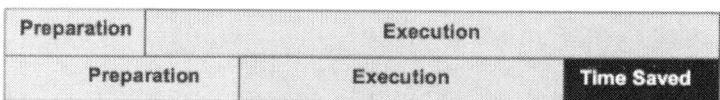

Time well invested in *additional* preparation is repaid "with interest" in execution, and therefore *saves time*. To benefit from this, we need to *refuse to be diverted* by apparent urgency (our own or others'), by personal "comfort" or by avoiding "difficult" situations.

Preparation is the key to effectiveness and enjoyment and to creating time, space and freedom from stress.

Knowing how to prepare well is the most important leadership skill, and *questions* are the key to good preparation (see FF 4-6 for levels and first examples).

Only *you* can decide how much or how *well* you prepare!

Fault 8:
Change or Growth?

We may tend to think of change as structural and growth as strategic. Newly appointed leaders wishing to show they are having an impact like to make rapid changes in management or organizational *structures*.

The phrase *Managing Change* has itself come to refer primarily to structural changes – usually disruptive – in response to crises that are likely the fruit of passive leadership in the past.

Growth similarly tends to be visualized quantitatively, such as in metrics of increased employee numbers, market penetration or financial revenues.

To free ourselves of this change/growth duality and come to something more real and immediate, we need to see *growth* as the antithesis of *decay,* and to see *change* as *qualitative* movements between them.

Changes towards decay happen naturally and easily over time. Changes away from decay and towards growth require sustained effort that is both intentional and ever more conscious. This applies equally for individuals, teams, organizations, communities and governments.

Fix 8:
Raise *Leadership Mindset!*

While structural and strategic changes do not initially require qualitative changes in leadership capability, the changes needed for cultural growth cannot be achieved without development of leadership *mindset.*

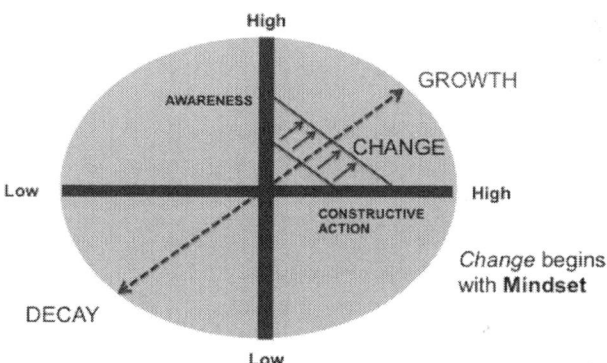

Change begins with **Mindset**

Leadership and cultural growth require intentional efforts towards *balanced increases* in awareness and constructive action. To the dictum of the 1980's that "structure follows strategy" we can add: *"strategy follows culture."*

The "change" line between decay and growth can also represent improvement or deterioration of *attitude.*

Fault 9:
Agree or Disagree?

We tend to assume that we see things "as they really are" and that if others see things differently then they are "wrong." This is the essence of judging in Mindset Levels +1 and -1.

Through such assumptions we ignore the fact that we *interpret* the outside world through what we might call a "filter" unique to each of us.

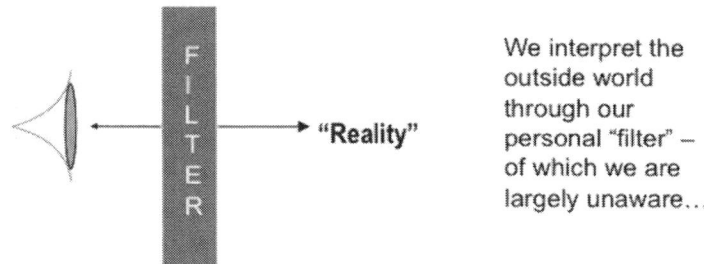

"Reality"

We interpret the outside world through our personal "filter" – of which we are largely unaware...

To work towards level +2, we need to remember that we are largely unaware of our "filters," and then to communicate accordingly. Through our "filters" we judge quickly, especially new people or ideas, branding them as positive or negative.

In particular we judge *ourselves* by our *intentions*, and *others* by their *actions*! And they do the same!

Fix 9:
Study *Reactions!*

To start moving from passive to dynamic mindsets, we need to develop an interest in observing both our own and others' "filters."

We can find out most easily about our own "filters" from studying our own intellectual, emotional and physical intelligence (FF 11-20 of this book).

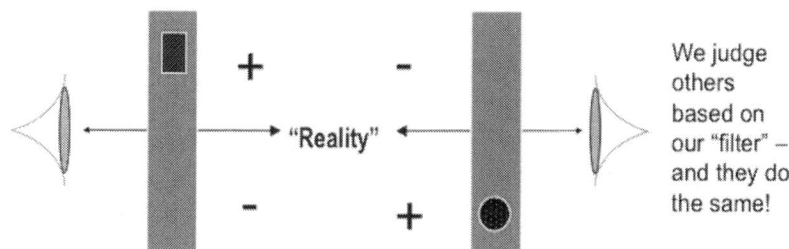

And we can find out most easily about other people's "filters." especially those in our 360 relationships, through our interactions with them (see FF 21-30).

The most valuable learning can come from developing the habit of *witnessing our own inner reactions* where there are different "filters," as pictured above (see FF 18-19).

Fault 10:
Courses or Books?

By definition, we don't and *cannot* know the path of our own personal development.

When we review how we developed in the past – whether in leadership or in intentionally acquiring any other skill or capability – we see that typically there was a *process* that was probably not visible to us until after it was completed.

This development process is very often a progression from the uncertainty of *relative passivity (+1)* in the chosen field to the learning and improvement of relative *activity (+2)* and then to the relative expertise, confidence and continuous learning of *creativity (+3)*.

It needs to include *new experience* resulting from *creative inner questioning*, which may or may not be stimulated or accelerated by a book, course, teacher, guide, coach or senior leader.

The broader question of Measuring and Transforming leadership will occupy us through FF 51-60. For now let's try to visualize the process of continuous learning that is the hallmark of level +3 mindsets.

Fix 10:
Conduct *Live* Research!

A level +3 leader is *constantly* looking out for and seeing, in numerous contexts, areas of relative passivity (-1 and +1) and striving to bring them to +2 and +3.

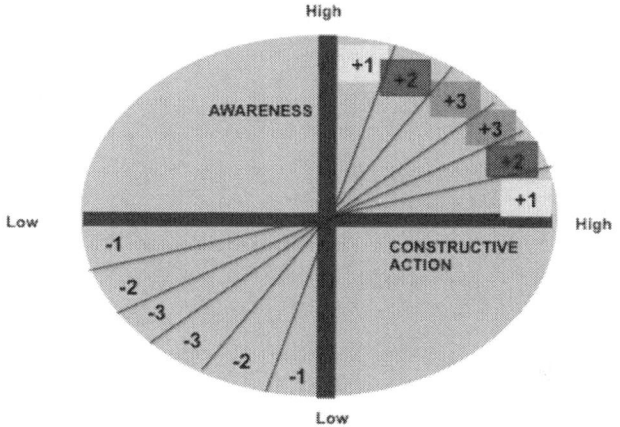

This habit needs to be developed and applied first to our own mindsets and intelligence levels; this is where we can first learn the principles of developing mindset.

As these principles become clearer we can more easily and effectively apply them in our roles as leaders of teams and organizations and also as citizens, constructively influencing the culture around us.

Leadership Faults & Fixes

Threefold Intelligence

Our IQ, EQ and PQ – intellectual, emotional, and physical intelligence – are the *sources* and at the same time the *components* of our mindset.

Through their separate and combined action every day, these three types of intelligence underpin and limit our leadership and culture. In much, perhaps most, of human experience, each type of intelligence works in *dualities*.

Faults 11-20 reveal aspects and examples of each type of intelligence that have the potential, even the need, to develop throughout life and so to transcend dualities that limit them.

The underlying theory that emerges is not to be blindly believed but rather to be tested in practice.

For each Fault, the accompanying Fix aims to expand awareness around the topic, with in some cases suggestions for such testing.

Fault 11:
Intelligent or Unintelligent?

It seems natural to think and say that human beings are intelligent, to question whether other animals are also intelligent and to speculate on the existence of "intelligent life" in other parts of the universe.

In the secret services, "intelligence" often means *information*, while in everyday speech its apparent absence is often seen as a lack of "common sense."

Our knowledge of *types* of intelligence is limited and may be theoretical rather than practical. We can be amused by the idea that a "brilliant" professor can be absent-minded, unaware that in some cultures an absent-minded person is seen as far from intelligent.

As leaders we need to come to know in ourselves and recognize in others *three types of intelligence* – IQ (intellectual), EQ (emotional) and PQ (physical) – and to become aware of *levels* within each type and of our daily *oscillations and fluctuations* between levels.

Focusing on levels of IQ, EQ and PQ, and also how *each type of intelligence impacts the other two*, can help us envision how mindset can be developed.

Fix 11:
See *Levels* of Intelligence!

The diagram below shows key words to give a taste of each of the three types of intelligence. It's important to note that these key words are just that – *not definitions!*

Key Words for each of the Six Levels of Quality				
Level	Mindset	IQ	EQ	PQ
+3	Constructive Inclusion	Objective Thought	Unconditional Feelings	Full Vitality, Presence
+2	Constructive Dynamism	Constructive Thought	Constructive Passions	Constructive Appetites
+1	Constructive Passivity	Positive Associations	Likes; Positive Reactions	Positive Tensions
-1	Destructive Passivity	Negative Associations	Dislikes; Negative Reactions	Negative Tensions
-2	Destructive Dynamism	Destructive Thoughts	Destructive Passions	Destructive Appetites
-3	Destructive Exclusion	Fragmented Thoughts	Emotional Prison	Impaired or Ruined Vitality

Much of human life is *contained within and fluctuates between* levels -2, -1, +1 and +2, as shown in products of popular culture such as soap operas.

Suggestion: Take 10 minutes to contemplate each type of intelligence and find your own examples and further key words that help flesh out the six levels of each.

Fault 12:
Like or Dislike?

Our "like" and "dislike" of objects, of events and of other people are examples of our positive and negative emotional reactions at EQ Levels +1 and -1.

Such reactions permeate daily life. In social media, they are invited, sought and expressed. They give material for discussions and gossip, and provide evidence for subtler evaluations, such as of " taste."

Where they come from is more mysterious. Are they really "ours," or have we copied them? Based on memories or fashions? Consequently a prejudice?

Like other Level 1 emotional, intellectual and physical reactions, there can be *oscillation* between +1 and -1; for example, an idea or person that was initially liked can sooner or later be disliked, and vice-versa.

Often we like or dislike people based on conscious or unconscious *expectations* of how we think or feel *they should behave towards us*. This is important for leaders, who may have to lead people they don't like!

How to reduce potentially negative effects of "like" and "dislike"?

Fix 12:
Create *Intent!*

The energy of Level -1 emotions such as dislike and, very importantly, *fear,* can be harnessed to generate *aspirations* that lift mindsets towards Level +2.

This can be achieved by using creative questions such as those in FF6 to generate formulations of *purpose* (the contribution upwards), and *aims* (downwards and peer).

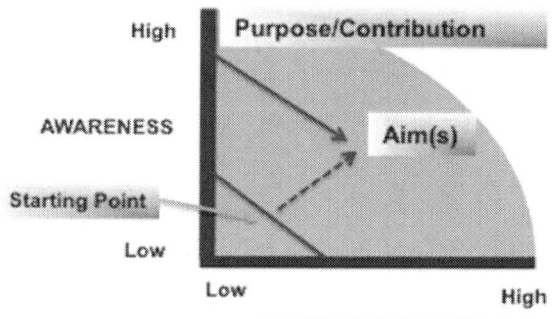

Formulating intent as purpose and aims, *connected to relationships,* can temporarily transform EQ Level 1 energies

This generation and expression of *intent* can achieve at least temporary transcending of Level 1 EQ.

A more lasting EQ shift requires *grounding* of aims so that they can come to fruition, and this in turn requires inputs from IQ and PQ (see FF 13-14).

Fault 13:
Yes or No?

In intellectual intelligence (IQ), Level 1 comprises our ability to register, categorize and file associations and memories generated through experience.

Together with the rich and varied components of EQ Levels +1 and -1, such as likes and dislikes, fears and corresponding comforts, our memories and mental associations build up what becomes a treasure-chest of more or less organized impressions and interpretations of experience and ways of interacting with the world.

This process, which happens through our childhood and youth, produces what we call our *personality* – from the Latin word *persona*, meaning "mask." It may be guided by intentional input from family or teachers, or it may develop haphazardly without conscious influence – for most of us, probably a mixture.

Leaders with Mindset Level 1 (which includes +1 and -1) think, decide and communicate from *personality*. They can be found in all kinds of organizations, businesses, professional firms and governments.

In developing *beyond* personality, we start to become aware of and free from our habitual yeses and noes.

Fix 13:
Translate Intent *into Metrics!*

Just as Level 1 EQ can be harnessed to generate *intent* (see FF12), so Level 1 IQ can be focused to Level +2 to generate *metrics* through which fruition of purpose and aims can be mentally projected into the future.

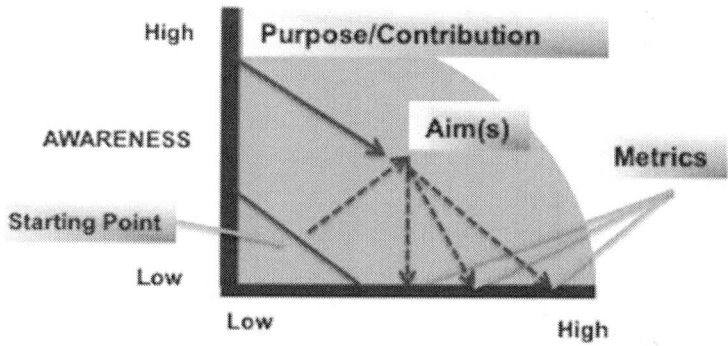

Formulating and *connecting intent and metrics* requires a blend of Level +2 EQ and IQ and that is one of many reasons why level 1 planning is routinely ineffective and may become uninteresting. Clarity of terminology is important too: *aims* are developmental or aspirational; *metrics* are **concrete** indicators that are measureable over time. (Note: "goals" and "objectives" are often unconsciously used for either *aims* or *metrics* or both.)

Fault 14:
Tense or Relaxed?

We cannot be consciously aware of the extraordinary intelligence that regulates the functioning of our physical organism, from the nervous, circulatory and metabolic systems to life at cellular level.

What we *can* become more aware of, and influence intentionally, are the *conditions* in which they operate, through our interest, for example, in health, fitness and quality of nutrition. This is the first focus of Leadership PQ (physical intelligence).

At Level 1 of PQ, corresponding to the memories and associations of IQ and the likes and dislikes of EQ, we can become more aware of and study *tensions* – primarily muscular tensions, also psychic tensions. Both types of tension connect to EQ and IQ.

Level +1 tensions are *needed*, for example for a task to be performed. To lift a shopping bag requires a tensing of certain arm, finger and perhaps shoulder muscles. It does *not* require a grimace or other facial tension, which in this context is a level -1 tension.

As with EQ and IQ, there can be oscillation between levels +1 and -1 that can waste available energy.

Fix 14:
Get *Grounded!*

In leadership thinking just as with electricity, the dual "currents" of IQ and EQ need to be *grounded* by PQ, otherwise there will be *static* – no change or movement!

PQ Level +2 features *constructive appetites* including the appetite for *new action*. First, we need to work to remove unnecessary (-1) tensions, which can also come from Level -1 EQ and IQ, so that we become *grounded*.

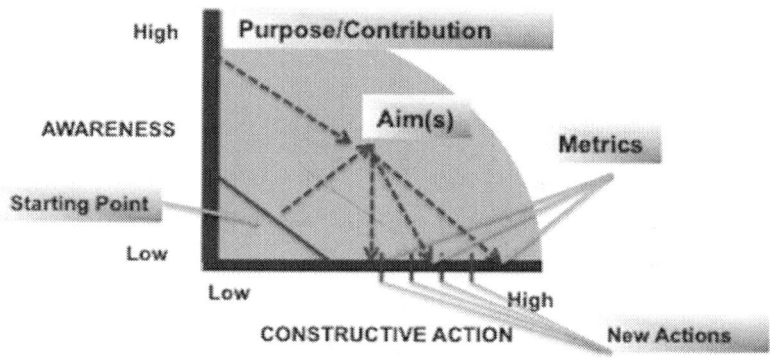

In leadership mindset, this grounding shows in the creation of new action towards new metrics. This means flexibility and adaptability away from habitual activities, which otherwise form negative tensions that tend to pull +2 EQ and +2 IQ back to Level +1 and -1.

Fault 15:
Love or Hate?

The world of Level +2 in emotional intelligence (EQ) is the world of *conditional passions*.

We are familiar with these in, for example, the type of "love" that can fluctuate to "hate" and back again, and in constructive commitments of all kinds that become destructive when explicit or implicit conditions are not met. We see them at the theatre and permeating life.

Since the movements between +2 and -2 tend to be less frequent and more dramatic than those between +1 and -1, we can refer to them as *fluctuations* rather than *oscillations*. Further examples: a movement between confidence (+2) and arrogance (-2), or the change of energy when a competitive sports game suddenly erupts into a fight between two or more players. Here the Level +2 energy of *constructive dynamism* has fluctuated "downwards" to the *destructive dynamism* of Level -2.

Level -2 is the level of violence in all contexts. It can come as a fluctuation from Level +2 or as a developed extension of -1. In IQ it takes the form of destructive thoughts and arguments, in EQ violent passions.

So what is meant by Levels +3 and -3 in EQ?

Fix 15:
Get Free from *Inner Conditions!*

EQ Level -3 features enslavement to negative emotions.

EQ Level +3 is a very different world – the world of true *feelings* (not emotional reactions) that *have no opposites* but are simply present or absent: patience, joy, gratitude, unconditional love, compassion…

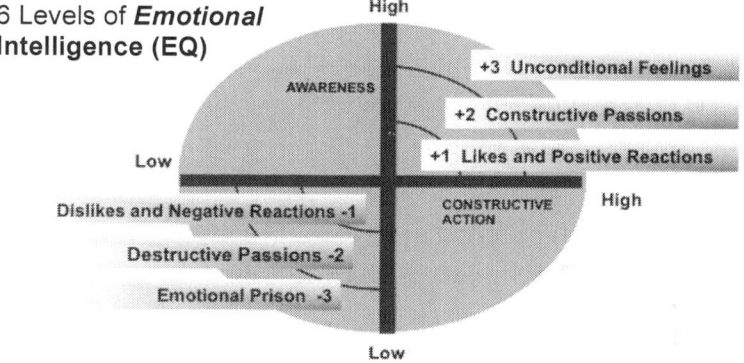

In each type of intelligence (IQ, EQ and PQ), Levels +3 and -3 are much more rare than the other levels. And very importantly, they *don't oscillate or fluctuate* from one to the other; Level +3 can only *emerge* from Level +2, and Level -3 is formed only as a *descent* from Level -2.

FF 18-19 give first indications on moving from +2 to +3.

Fault 16:
Right or Wrong?

Quick judgments of "right" and "wrong," such as on questions of factual correctness, are examples of IQ level +1 and -1 reactions.

The imprecision of language means that these terms can also refer to legal, moral or ethical questions, in which arguments and lines of reasoning are more complex.

IQ Levels +2 and -2 feature our capacity to compare and contrast information and ideas and to create strong and compelling arguments for (+2) or against (-2) particular causes or conclusions. Here the data of levels +1 and -1 become dynamic in energy and form.

As with emotional intelligence, IQ levels +1 and -1 can oscillate and levels +2 and -2 can fluctuate, such as in a courtroom, debating chamber or negotiation where opposing arguments are presented (whether or not actually *believed* by those presenting them).

IQ level -2 can pass "downwards" to the -3 world of unresolvable arguments or mental delusion. IQ level +2 has the potential to be transformed "upwards" to level +3 where there is *relative* objectivity.

Fix 16:
Develop *Threefoldness!*

The intellectual shift from IQ Levels +1 and +2 towards +3 requires *threefoldness* in three key areas.

Since only the IQ can distinguish the threefoldness of *past, present and future,* it *must* first actualize itself by doing this, mentally separating them from each other.

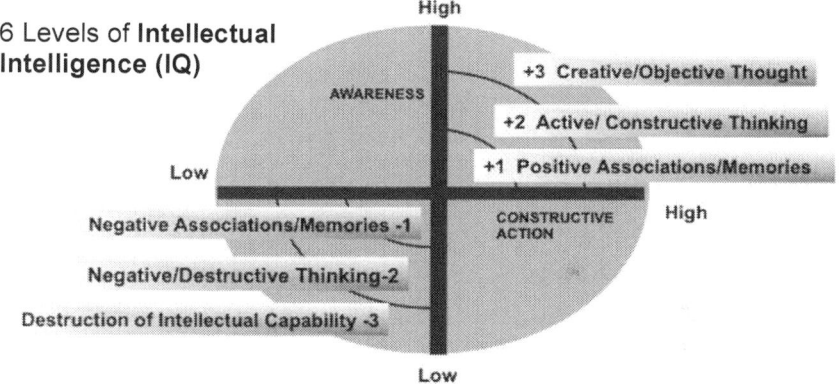

6 Levels of Intellectual Intelligence (IQ)

High

AWARENESS

+3 Creative/Objective Thought

+2 Active/ Constructive Thinking

+1 Positive Associations/Memories

Low

Negative Associations/Memories -1

Negative/Destructive Thinking-2

Destruction of Intellectual Capability -3

CONSTRUCTIVE ACTION

High

Low

Then, as seen in FF 12-14, it needs to work with the EQ and IQ in a threefold combination that in turn produces a threefold output: a formulation connecting *qualitative* needs (aims), *quantitative* measurements (metrics) and *diarized* actions for realization. All three are necessary for intentional change in any context!

Fault 17:
Good or Bad Appetites?

In everyday language a "good" or "bad" appetite is a simple IQ +1 or -1 judgment as to whether or not the initial part of the digestive process is working well.

The development of strong physical appetites – to do with *digestion* and also other aspects including *exercise* – connects to the development of PQ levels +2 and -2, and in this context "good" and "bad" refer to their impact, constructive or destructive, on *vitality*.

Here too we can see connections between the three types of intelligence. Genuinely constructive PQ appetites have a positive and noticeable impact on IQ and EQ.

Wrong IQ assumptions about "fitness" can *damage* vitality, immediately or subsequently, while intentional or unintentional disinformation (increasingly common in nutrition) is a -2 IQ and even EQ influence that easily generates -2 PQ appetites.

The often-unseen development of negative PQ appetites leads over time to impaired or ruined vitality (-3), also affecting EQ and IQ negatively.

Fix 17:
Generate *Vitality!*

It's important for leaders to demonstrate full physical vitality, both as part of their immediate presence and influence and as a component of leadership example.

This means discriminating carefully within received habits as well as new fads to find genuine information.

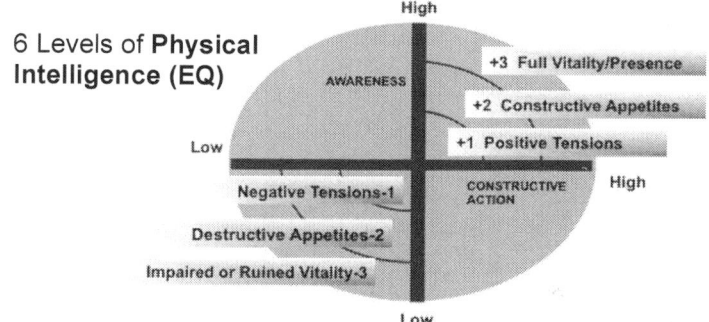

To develop our PQ, EQ and IQ, we need to identify and study live examples of our own and others' levels within the three types and how these inter-connect.

Suggestion: as an exercise to apply FF16 and connect your EQ, IQ and PQ, try to formulate a *metric* and a *diarized action* for the aim of *raising your own vitality!*

Fault 18:
Free Will or Fate?

In each of the three types of intelligence, IQ, EQ and PQ, our "center of gravity" has to become established at Level +2 before we can move to Level +3.

Our "center of gravity" means the level at which, day in day out, each type of intelligence typically operates within us. The 6 levels outlined through FF 11-17 give initial orientation; as we study more we can see that each level is itself an inner "world" of mindset, with multiple further levels within it.

As explored in FF5, we need to take care that our ability to envision, aspire towards or occasionally experience higher levels doesn't give us a false impression that this is *already* our center of gravity. We may, for example, fail to discriminate adequately between *will*, a very highly evolved feature of Level +3 intellectual intelligence that *has to be developed,* with *willfulness,* which is an unconscious -2 characteristic.

Life lived at Levels -3 up to +1 is relatively haphazard and can be ruled by chance influences, not least our own ungrounded imagination. To go higher, *ideas* of levels must give way to *witnessing* them.

Fix 18:
Observe the Filter!

To move from the +2 world of *constructive dynamism* – passions, drives, arguments and appetites – to the +3 world of *constructive inclusion* (see FF11) requires constant and rigorous *observation* of the formation and expression of our own inner and outer reactions. *Seeing* them helps us to stop *being* them!

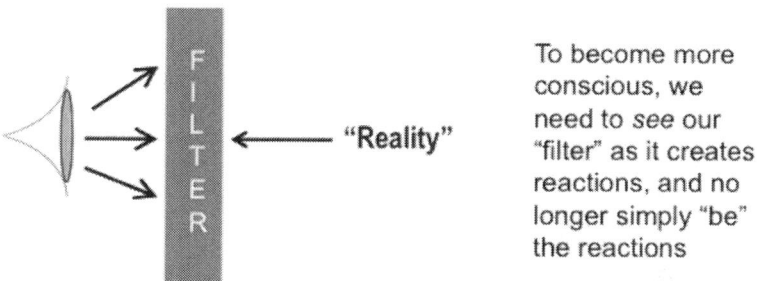

To become more conscious, we need to *see* our "filter" as it creates reactions, and no longer simply "be" the reactions

This is not easy because our emotional and physical reactions tend to work faster and more strongly than the *initially intellectual* idea of trying to witness them.

At first, we may only be able to observe reactions in hindsight. *Witnessing* them, we are *simultaneously aware* of an external event and our reaction to it.

For a moment, the duality of FF9 is transcended.

Fault 19:
Yes... BUT!

In most if not all languages, every day, one of the most common starts to a phrase or sentence is the expression: "Yes, but..." You may even have been saying it internally to yourself now and again while reading this book!

We naturally wish to acknowledge – that is, to say "yes" by way of validating – what another person says or writes, especially if it's someone we already *like!*

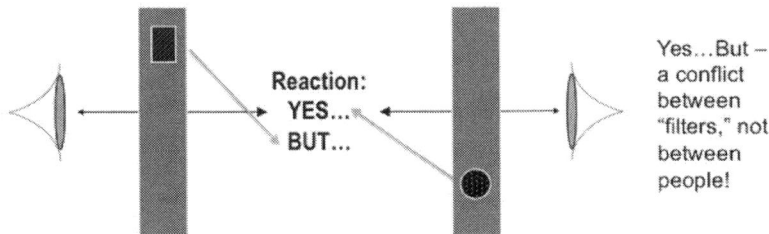

Reaction:
YES...
BUT...

Yes...But –
a conflict
between
"filters," not
between
people!

The challenge to this is our *inability to reconcile* what has been said or written with the existing contents of our "filter" (see FF 9 and 18). A contradiction results, and a negative, even violent, argument may ensue.

Suggestion: when witnessing your own "Yes...buts" try changing the *but* to *and*, followed by a *question!*

Fix 19:
Use Personality as *Food!*

The simple technique of substituting "and" for "but," making the "Yes!" real and moving from past to future with a question, gives a glimpse of the *attitude* that is a hallmark of a Level +3 mindset as it grows.

The continuous effort of focusing attention to *include and transcend* our own and others' reactions gives a pathway to the emergence of Level +3 intelligence.

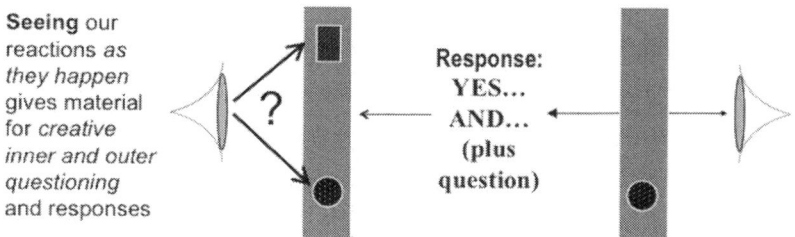

Seeing our reactions *as they happen* gives material for *creative inner and outer questioning* and responses

?

Response:
YES...
AND... ◄
(plus question)

Level +3 intelligence has to be *built*. The materials are fashioned from our personality – the accumulated deposits of our "filter" over the years – and our main building tool is our own, strengthening, inner focus.

The product: a new *substance* which, translating directly from the Latin root, we can call: *understanding!*

Fault 20:
Heaven or Hell?

The energy of intellectual intelligence that we refer to as *attention* varies in quantity and quality.

In Levels -3 to +1, the quantity of attention is deficient, and those lacking their own attention may do everything to attract and use that of others.

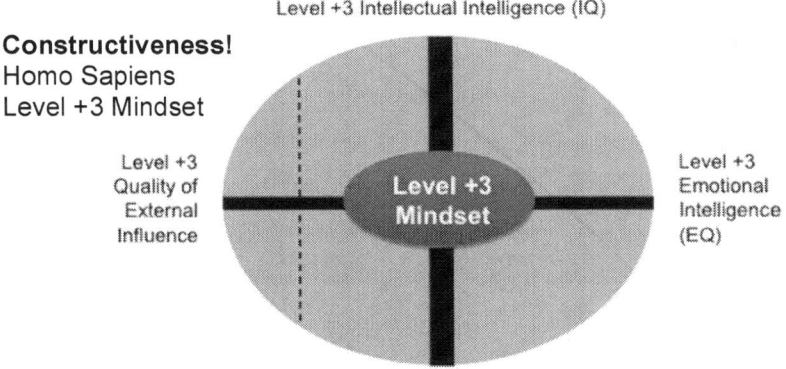

The attention of Level +2 is *intentionally directed* and, when strong, can carry the effort needed to develop the possibilities, habits and focus outlined in FF 19.

This is what is necessary for *understanding* to grow.

Fix 20:
Acknowledge *Commonality!*

As we contemplate intelligence, two pictures come into view representing humankind's ultimate duality.

They show the twin pillars of *constructiveness* (+3) and *(self-)destructiveness* (-3) of the intelligence and mindset of a species calling itself *Homo Sapiens!*

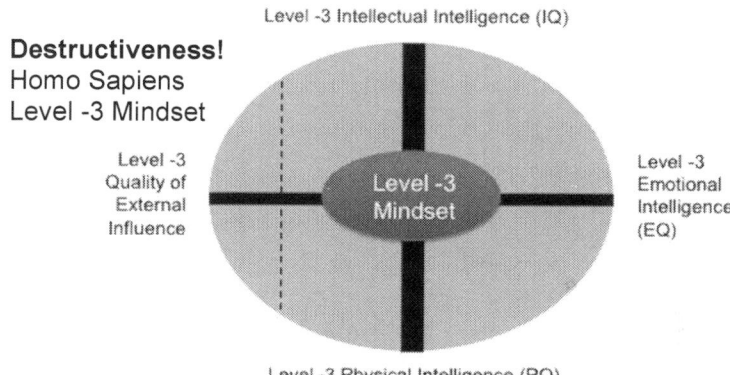

Within these +3 and -3 extremes, the center of gravity of our species hovers between -2, -1, +1 and +2 (see FF11).

This is where leadership attention has its calling!

Communicating as a Leader

In FF 1-20 we have established that leaders have 3 key types of internal relationship, the quality of which impact external influence.

The quality of these internal relationships (higher, lower, peer) depends on the quality of *mindset*, which itself has 3 inner components: IQ, EQ and PQ.

In FF 21-30 we'll see how levels of *mindset* determine the quality of *communication* through the core interactions that underpin 360 relationships.

In the vertical relationships, the leader is the interface connecting organizational needs to individual aspirations. Through the horizontal relationships, leaders connect internal peer groups with external entities, such as clients.

The resulting quality of 360 relationships shapes and spreads organizational culture.

Fault 21:
Hire or Reject?

The quality of hiring is the *first key influence* on the quality of team performance and organizational culture.

Under leadership mindsets -2 and -3 (see FF2), hiring can be haphazard, driven by crisis or by the *personal* interests of the leader. New hires may find their arrival on the first day is a surprise to those around them!

Passive leadership cultures (Level -1 and +1) aim to maintain the status quo, focusing on a candidate's CV, qualifications and similarity to existing staff. The hiring process normally excludes exposure to prospective new colleagues, and there is minimal induction.

In Level +2, selection criteria are pre-established and external agencies may be used; attention is given to making the organization appear attractive, and there may be multiple contacts prior to a decision, with testing of *attitude* and *capability to perform*. There is a planned induction process. Level +2 *includes and transcends* +1.

Level +3 approaches similarly include and transcend +2, with key differences concerning both *diversity* and *how roles are defined*.

Fix 21:
Define Roles *Creatively!*

Level +1 role definitions are typically lists of activities; Level +2 includes performance goals without connection to broader aims and purpose. Level +3 hiring specifies *why* the role is needed, what its purpose/contribution is to be and *how* its core relationships are to be conducted.

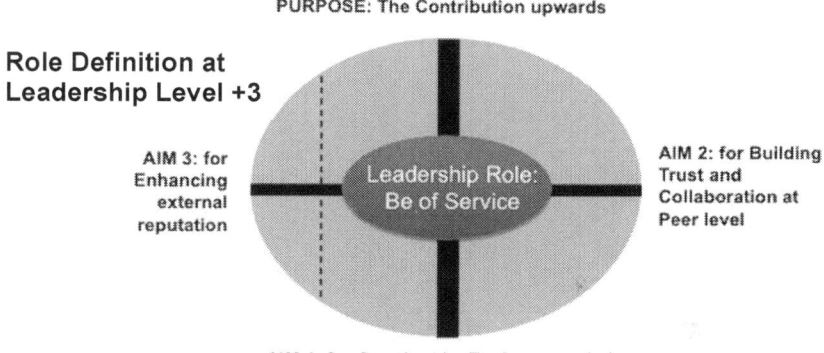

PURPOSE: The Contribution upwards

Role Definition at Leadership Level +3

AIM 3: for Enhancing external reputation

Leadership Role: Be of Service

AIM 2: for Building Trust and Collaboration at Peer level

AIM 1: for Creating the Environment below

This broad role definition is developed in the hiring process and made concrete on take-up (with reviewable metrics and actions – see FF14).

Diversity is *structural* at Level +1, *performance- driven* at Level +2, and *intelligence-based* at Level +3.

Fault 22:
Delegate or Hoard?

The quality of delegating is the *second key influence* on team performance and organizational culture.

Under leadership mindsets -1, -2 and -3, *responsibility* is offloaded, while *power* is retained. At levels +1, +2 and +3, there are different degrees of *empowerment*, while overall responsibility is never relinquished.

In passive leadership cultures (Level -1 and +1), work is delegated as a reaction to energy levels or time constraints; the delegator gives *instructions* ("do me a favor") about what to do *and how to do it*, without planned follow-up ("come back if there's a problem"). In professional firms, Level 1 features a reticence to allow direct contact with ("my") clients.

In Level +2, there is dialogue! The delegator prepares and communicates *goals* and delegates *thinking* for the path to the goal, recognizing that this can promote new and better ideas, engagement, and time saving.

Level +2 also includes planned follow-up, and there may be an interval before the delegated work starts for the team member to plan, perhaps involving others.

Fix 22:
Empower!

In Level +3 *decision-making* is delegated to the lowest level possible, with regular informal reviews and a focus on learning.

Sample preparation questions for a mindset Level +3 delegation interaction:

• What are the needs of the organization/team here?

• Why are these needs important, and how can I make sure the delegatee appreciates them?

• What empowerment opportunities are available here? What's blocking *further* empowerment?

• What *learning* is implied? How can I assist it? What do I need to find out from the delegatee?

• What is *non-negotiable* in this work/project, and where is there room/need for new thinking?

• What *positive* references can open the dialogue?

• What *preparation* shall I *request*?

Suggestion: Reflect on a recent delegation interaction. At what leadership mindset level was it prepared and conducted? What possibilities do you see for raising the game here?

Fault 23:
Review or Not?

The quality of reviewing is the *third key influence* on team performance and organizational culture.

Under mindsets -1, -2 and -3, this meeting does not exist. If there is feedback on performance or behavior, it is vague, one-way *negative* criticism, with the leader expressing *personal* dissatisfaction and even threat.

In Level +1 leadership cultures, the fact that the meeting takes place is seen as an achievement. If it does happen, it's exclusively about the *past*, with the reviewer doing *all or most* of the talking and *passing judgment* on the reviewee. Neither party looks forward to the meeting and it typically generates *defensiveness*.

In Level +2, there is dialogue that includes the *future!* Both parties are *prepared*, and the reviewer's goal is that the reviewee leaves the meeting *motivated* towards new intent or actions planned during it.

In Level +3, the constant flow of formal and informal review dialogues constitutes a *living process* for aligning and re-aligning aspirations, performance and learning with organizational and client needs.

Fix 23:
Connect *Needs* to *Aspirations!*

Sample preparation questions for a mindset Level +3 performance review meeting:

- What are the needs of the organization/team here?
- Which are already met/being met?
- What concrete evidence supports this?
- What is needed next?
- What do I already know of the team member's learning and aspirations?
- How to find out more?
- What do I need to make sure the team member understands by the end of the meeting?
- What will indicate that this has been achieved?
- How can I help the team member create or renew a positive self-image of capability and potential?

At Level +3, the quality of influence is continuously in focus. Moments such as a cab ride following a client interaction are seized as opportunities to review and renew the quality of impact, perhaps later confirmed by a short email from one or other party as a guide to the next such interaction.

Fault 24:
Confront or Avoid?

The quality of reprimand, or correction and re-alignment of performance, is the *fourth key influence* on team performance and organizational culture.

In mindsets -1, -2 and -3, this meeting is avoided until there is a crisis. In -3 it will likely end the relationship; in -2 lead to a major argument. In a -1 culture it will mean the creation of "dead wood" and a negative influence on morale and performance (see FF37).

In a level +1 culture, it will again either be avoided or, if addressed, done so in a tentative way where the priority might be to avoid any upset. This can result in dancing around the situation rather than resolving it.

It's only in level +2 and +3 cultures that poor performance or attitude is addressed constructively. This is made constructive by creating *an inner duality in the mind of the other person* between what is conceptually desirable (or previously agreed) and what has actually happened, resulting in an inner conflict for resolution and *increased understanding.*

If the confrontation becomes *externalized*, there may easily be a fluctuation from +2 to -2.

Fix 24:
Create *Inner* Confrontation!

This inner duality is typically created with 3 elements: a +1 question to check understanding of the principle at stake (see FF4), a level +1 or +2 question to verify what happened, and +3 questions to generate understanding and solutions, with concrete arrangements for follow up.

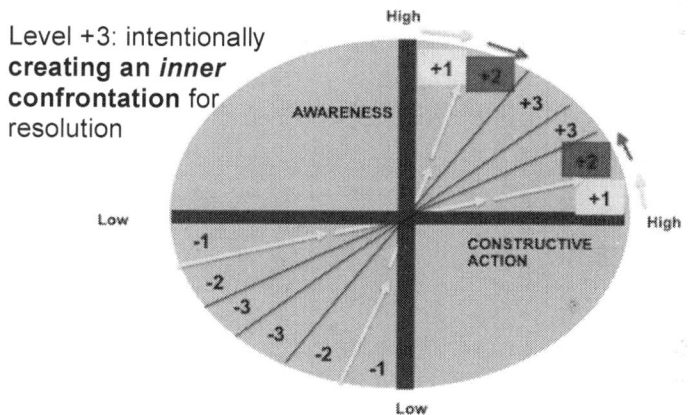

Level +3: intentionally **creating an *inner* confrontation for** resolution

Through such questions, and by acknowledging and building on the other's responses, the +3 leader eliminates negativity and *facilitates* a shift in mindset from destructive to constructive and from passive to dynamic. In Level +3 cultures, this becomes a routine approach for *creating and renewing operating principles.*

Fault 25:
Complain or Leave Alone?

The way in which we deal with *perceived failings by those in higher authority* is a *fifth key* influence on the quality of team and organizational culture.

In level -2 and -3 cultures, such perceptions are not tolerated and they are therefore not expressed. In Level -1, they may be occasionally expressed, typically in the form of complaints. Since complaints are perceived as negative, they will tend to generate defensiveness and resistance, unless there is level +2 or +3 listening.

In Level +1, complaints are avoided as they risk the perception of undermining the status quo. (They will be more acceptable if the complaint is about something that may itself undermine the status quo.)

In Level +2, the complaints are *transformed in the mindset of the complainer*, so that they are expressed as improvements or solutions from the point of view of the higher authority/internal client.

In Level +3, leaders are quietly active in detecting areas of dissatisfaction and in subtly addressing them.

Fix 25:
Recommend *Change!*

How to make the transition from a negative and potentially destructive *impulse to complain* to a positive and constructive *wish to help and improve?*

To help make this internal adjustment of *attitude*, we can benefit from questions that foster both emotional and intellectual *preparation*, such as:

- What are the main goals or wishes of the senior?
- How could the change I'm looking for be of value to him/her towards achieving/satisfying these goals?
- What is the exact change I want, and by when?
- What could be a first, simple *action* for them to say "yes!" to?
- What additional benefits are there?
- How can I make it easy for the person to say "Yes"?
- What opening question might best create interest?

This is not a matter of a Level -2 subservience; it is a way of creatively serving a need of higher authority.

If the higher authority seems to misunderstand their *own* needs, then the approach of FF24 may be appropriate.

Fault 26:
Difficult Clients or Colleagues?

Vertical interactions tend initially to receive greater attention and focus than *horizontal*. In FF 21-25 we have explored ways in which the quality of mindset impacts key vertical interactions.

At levels below a +2 leadership mindset, the quality of *horizontal* relationships can be *haphazard*. In peer relations within a professional firm, for example, there can be visible or invisible prejudices between practice areas, competitive internal promotions, and confusion in meeting differing requirements of seniors.

At Level +1, there may be momentum and reputation generated by predecessors through past client work, that maintains a certain level of peer group collaboration.

Level +2 leaders intentionally organize intact or virtual team members around work that generates *dynamic* collaboration; at Level +3 there is *creative connection* of peers and clients – such as in developing multi-level contacts and in cross selling.

Note: client relationships are placed as *horizontal* in the individual 360 because the difference in authority is part of the *organizational* 360 (see FF31).

Fix 26:
Align to Others' *Filters!*

An overview of variations in key client interactions:

Needs analysis
- *Level +1:* reliance on the client brief; focus on "rational" needs rather than emotional drivers;
- *Level +2:* articulation and inclusion of emotional drivers and requirements
- *Level +3:* client is assisted to expand awareness of own needs and future challenges

Pitching and Presenting
- *Level +1:* against brief only; may be a standardized presentation; technical focus
- *Level +2:* based on revealed emotional/strategic needs and revealing specific tailored benefits
- *Level +3:* interactive and fully tailored to client's perspective, reflected in the smallest details

Handling Client Complaints
- *Level +1:* avoided and/or negative/defensive
- *Level +2:* acknowledged; addressed constructively
- *Level +3:* actively sought and welcomed as a source of information and ideas for service improvement

Fault 27:
Meeting or Preaching?

Team and group meetings are among the highest financial investments an organization makes.

In organizations of all kinds, the "senior management team" may be anything but a team, with each "team member" focused on managing their own part of the organization and paying lip service to team meetings.

In Level -1 mindsets, there can also be a prevalence of defensiveness and past orientation so that decision-making only happens if there is a crisis. Level -2 meetings feature unproductive arguments, and at Level -3 there can be rambling speech by the "leader," with no-one recording or subsequently remembering the content.

Level +1 meetings are routine and built around a routine list of topics ("agenda"); the leader tends to speak more than others, and the follow-up "minutes" contain a detailed report of what was *said*.

At Level +2, meetings exist for generating decisions and action. The agenda takes the form of *questions*; all participants prepare and participate actively; only agreed actions and follow-up are recorded.

Fix 27:
Raise Mindset Levels!

Level +3 meetings are a process for creating unity out of diversity that is engaging and rewarding for all.

The leader's focus is on raising to at least Level +2 individual and collective mindsets around topics and areas currently at +1 level or lower.

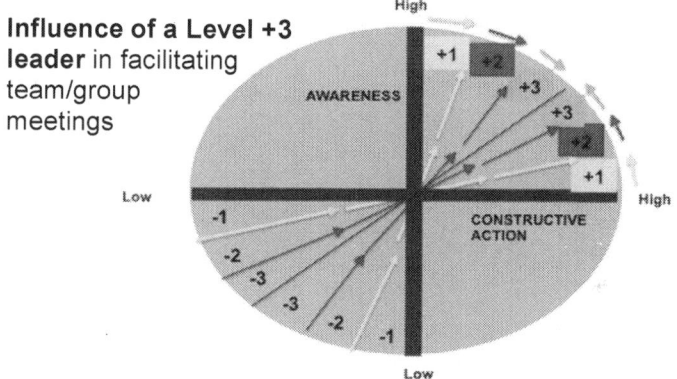

Influence of a Level +3 leader in facilitating team/group meetings

At Level +3, the leader becomes a skilled facilitator, constructively and subtly influencing the quality and *center of gravity* of IQ, EQ and PQ across the team.

Unity of focus is created through common interests that are not addressed at Level +2. For senior teams, these can include their combined influence on *culture*.

Fault 28:
Creative or Stuck?

The creative potential of a team or group begins with its combined capability to generate ideas. Leadership is needed to create the IQ, EQ and PQ environment for creativity and the most productive balance between divergent and convergent thinking

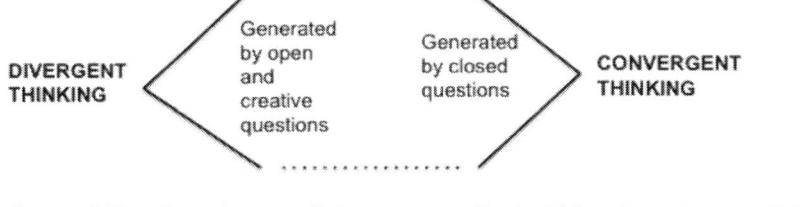

| DIVERGENT THINKING | Generated by open and creative questions | Generated by closed questions | CONVERGENT THINKING |

Start of Meetings (generally)...   End of Meetings (generally)...

The best-known type of interaction for this is called *brainstorming*, a term which usually refers to Phase 2 on the page opposite.

In Level +1 cultures and below, this meeting doesn't happen. In Level +2, it happens, based on questions prepared by the leader, though often descending to lower level (+1, -1, -2) discussions/arguments as suspension of judgment falters. In Level +3, it's part of the culture.

Fix 28:
Pre-Brainstorm!

The conventional (Level +2) "brainstorm" has two Phases, corresponding to Phases 2 and 3 shown below. In Level +3 cultures, Phase 1 below is added.

Phase 1 (Divergent thinking)

The leader guides a *pre-brainstorm* on the subject "What questions can we most usefully brainstorm?" generating a list of agreed questions to brainstorm.

Phase 2 (Divergent thinking)

Brainstorm of prepared questions, the leader adding additional sub-questions as may be helpful. The aim is to produce a list of ideas through a process of thought association. Judgment *must* be suspended so that the thought association process is not interrupted or broken.

(The difficulty of this suspension of judgment is the reason that many attempts at brainstorming fail and that it therefore does not enter the culture fully at level +2.)

Phase 3 (Convergent thinking)

Analysis leading to decision-making (this can be done at a different time or place and even by a different group).

Fault 29:
Win or Lose?

Negotiating is one of the most important interactionism leadership communication. It is the only interaction that features naturally in all three key internal relationships as well as in external communication.

The underlying premise of any negotiation is that both parties have a genuine wish for a solution or agreement. In leadership Levels -1, -2 and -3, such meetings don't happen because this premise is not met.

In Level +1 negotiation meetings, at least one party remains emotionally attached to entrenched positions that allow little or no movement. Such meetings become protracted and may end in stalemate. If there is an agreed solution, both parties may feel they have lost out.

In Level +2 there is a separation between past-oriented *positions* ("we have always done it this way..." "This belongs to us...") and future-oriented *interests* ("What we would like to achieve is...") which are brought into and add flexibility to the bargaining/trade-off discussion.

Level +2 can retain an element of -2 through a spoken or unspoken insistence that "for us to win, they must lose."

Fix 29:
Create *Joint Contribution!*

Level +3 negotiations are of a different order. They go beyond resolving past difficulties and result both in a mutually satisfactory ("win-win") solution and *also* in an agreement for dynamic *collaboration* going forward.

The past situation is resolved *as a by-product* of a creative process that produces outcomes not envisaged by either party prior to the meeting.

This is achieved through the process of Level +3 *brainstorming* set out in FF28 rather than through a conventional negotiation process, starting with a *pre-brainstorm* that may feature questions such as:

- What are our combined strengths and potential in the wider environment?
- What can we *jointly contribute* to this wider context in future? (for example: in businesses, the context of the industry or market; with nations, the international context or that of future generations)
- How can we now go about this? (full brainstorm producing aims, metrics and actions as per FF14 and resolving unhelpful aspects from the past)

Fault 30:
Dysfunctional Team or Group?

To initiate or revitalize the functioning of a team or group, the leader can benefit from helping the team to visualize itself by viewing *its own* 360 relationships and their impact (see diagram opposite), and then applying the series of questions from FF6.

Key Words indicating Differences in Interactions between Levels				
FF	Interactions	Level +1	Level +2	Level +3
21	Hiring/Role Definition	Passive	For Results	For Intelligence
22	Delegating	Reactive	Proactive	For Learning
23	Reviewing	Haphazard	For Results	For the Culture
24	Correcting	Avoided	Addressed	Ingrained
25	Complaining	Defensive	Proposing	Recommending
26	Clients	Routine	For Change	For Growth
27	Team Meetings	Speeches	Decisions	For the Culture
29	Brainstorming	Crisis Only	For Methods	For Innovation
29	Negotiating	Avoided	Win-Lose	Win-Win

Good team/group leadership means regularly renewing the center of gravity of mindsets. The essential medium for this is the set of nine interactions discussed in FF 21-29 and summarized in the table above.

The 6 levels of individual mindset studied in FF 2-3 also apply to group mindsets, and the sense of responsibility varies similarly (see FF53).

Fix 30:
Help the Team *Visualize* Itself!

Suggestion: after reading and reflecting on FF 1-29, think through and note your responses to the following questions (these can be useful later for FF 51-60):

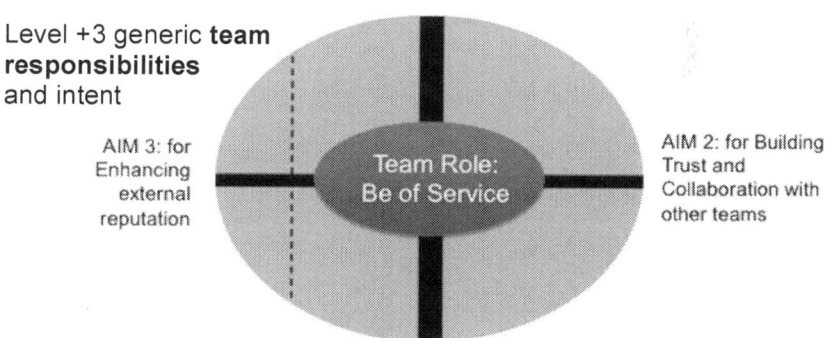

PURPOSE: The Contribution upwards (internal clients)

Level +3 generic **team responsibilities** and intent

AIM 3: for Enhancing external reputation

Team Role: Be of Service

AIM 2: for Building Trust and Collaboration with other teams

AIM 1: for Creating the Environment below for junior teams

- What do you see as the *center of gravity* of your own leadership mindset (see FF2)? How does it fluctuate?
- Similarly self-assess your current *center of gravity* in each type of intelligence (see FF11). Check with a close friend or partner if possible…
- What is the *center of gravity* of your leadership interactions (see diagram opposite)? Again, check with one or more team/group members…

Leadership Faults & Fixes

Organizations and Departments

In FF 1-30 we explored how different levels of Mindset and Intelligence impact the quality of a leader's Communication within his or her 360 set of relationships.

The quality of these relationships is vital: they take up most leadership time; through them the leader's reputation is created; and in combination with all other 360 interactions in an organization they make up the organization's culture.

Let's now see how the 6 levels of quality apply to the organization itself, within its own 360!

Fault 31:
Order or Chaos?

From time immemorial people have grouped or been grouped together whether as nomadic tribes, marauding armies or today's myriad business, governmental and social organizations that may comprise tens, hundreds, thousands, even hundreds of thousands of individuals.

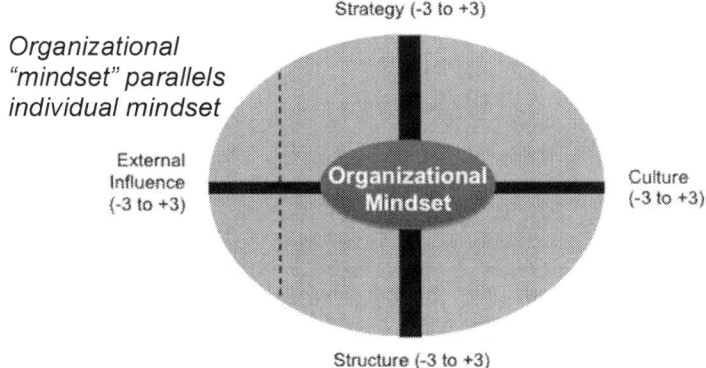

In terms of *quality* of organization, it can be helpful initially to make a parallel between organizational and individual *mindset* (see FF2 and FF20).

The IQ of an individual corresponds to organizational *strategy*, PQ to its *structure* and EQ to its *culture*, their combined quality similarly determining the quality of its impact and influence within its environment.

Fix 31:
See *Organizational* Quality!

We can connect the quality of individual mindset to *organizational* quality, using the same framework of six levels of awareness and constructive action already explored and applied through FF 1-30.

Key Words for each of the Six Levels of Quality			
Level	Mindset	Depts, BU's, PA's	Organization
+3	Constructive Inclusion	Joint Development of Culture	Creative Leadership of Industry
+2	Constructive Dynamism	Collaboration with other Depts, BU's, PA's	Strategy based on New Challenges/Goals
+1	Constructive Passivity	Routine Business & Procedures	Strategy based on Increments of Past
-1	Destructive Passivity	Distance from Other Depts, BU's, PA's	Only Structural Changes
-2	Destructive Dynamism	Silo Mentality; Unco-ordinated Business Dev	Politicking Internally
-3	Destructive Exclusion	Mutual Undermining of Effectiveness	Crisis

Suggestion: based on the key words indicated above for each of the levels -3 to +3, develop for yourself a fuller picture of an organization, department, business unit or practice area of interest to you.

What further characteristics, actual or potential, can you see or envision at each level? Where is there a noticeable center of gravity? What fluctuates between + and -?

Fault 32:
Hierarchical or Flat?

As seen in FF8, structure follows strategy and strategy follows culture. A jazz band may have a culture of spontaneity and self-determination that defines its (articulated or assumed) strategy of preferred types of gigs and audiences and therefore its structure in terms of vocal and instrumental musicians.

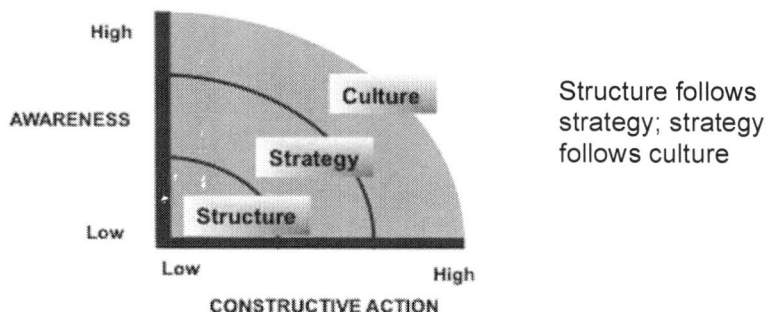

Structure follows strategy; strategy follows culture

If there is a "strategic" decision to expand the size of the band, this will only work if the culture allows it and can adapt to it – perhaps eventually with a chosen leader (conductor) and different sections of the expanded band, each with its own leader. Those who prefer the original culture may leave and form their own band; the new structure may need different musicians or personalities.

Fix 32:
See Organizational *Responsibility!*

Whether hierarchical or flat, organizations must *respond* to an external need to be viable. In this underlying sense of *responsibility*, there is again a direct parallel with the levels of leadership responsibility felt and acted upon by individuals (see FF3).

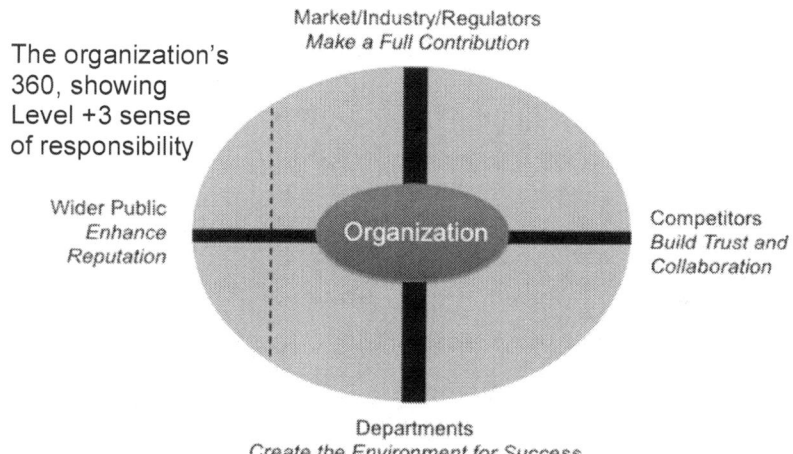

The organization's 360, showing Level +3 sense of responsibility

Market/Industry/Regulators
Make a Full Contribution

Wider Public
Enhance Reputation

Organization

Competitors
Build Trust and Collaboration

Departments
Create the Environment for Success

In Level +3 leadership Mindset, *strategy* connects the desired *contribution* to structure and activity. Note that the peer group (competitor) responsibility at Level +3 is to *build trust and collaboration*; the impulse to *compete aggressively* is part of Level +2 mindset.

Fault 33:
Strategy or No Strategy?

Many organizations, not least professional firms, tend to agonize over whether or not to "have" a strategy and, if they do formulate one, whether or not to publish it. The heart of the challenge is our tendency to think *tactically*, leading to confusion and inconsistency in understanding and using strategic terms.

In Level +3, strategic thinking means responding to the full set of creative questions – Why? What? How? How Much? Who? When? Where – in relation to the topic or activity in focus: a business, meeting, diet, holiday… The key terms are:

- **Vision** responding to "Why?" – often a concise expression of current or anticipated external *needs*
- **Mission** or **Purpose:** responding to "What?" and setting out the **Contribution** to be made
- **Aims** or **Intent** responding to "How?" and including *qualitative* elements for core relationships
- **Tactics** or **Actions:** responding to "Who?" "When?" Where?" and often taking the form of *communication*

In Levels +2 and +1, *vision* means *visualization* and *dream* respectively; in both, *strategy* means *tactics*.

Fix 33:
Be Strategic!

What's important is to apply strategic thinking, as just defined, to all leadership responsibilities and activities!

An organizational strategy in this sense is constructed similarly to a strategically thought-out role definition (see FF21). External communication will then take shape through the strategic thinking process.

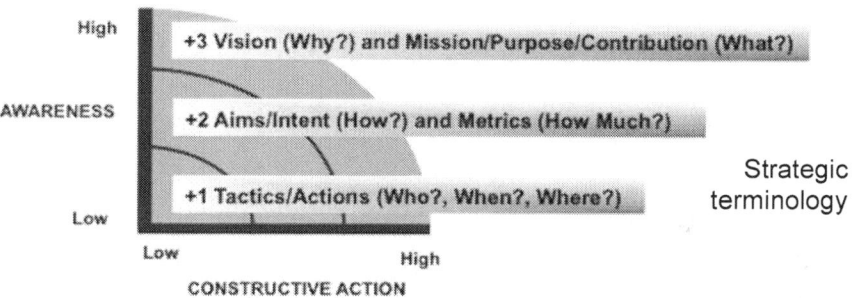

Suggestion: create from scratch a 1-page draft strategy for your organization (or your own part of it), applying the 360 diagram shown in FF32 and creating a *mission* for the relationship upwards (see FF6) and a statement of intent (aim) for each of the other relationships (see FF12) with metrics (FF13) and tactics/actions (FF14) for each.

What further input would you need to complete it?

Fault 34:
Values and Competencies?

Many organizations create and publish lists of (typically five to eight) "values" and/or a similar list of leadership "competencies" – in this case sometimes with different descriptions as to how they should apply in different roles within the organization's structure.

While it's important to be clear about what we stand for and also to have clear and consistent standards for performance, such lists are most typically found in +1 and +2 cultures where senior management has a concern about *quality*. On deeper analysis, the concern is over the *way* people operate and boils down to the quality of relationships and interactions.

The underlying difficulty with both is that managers lack the skill to connect such concepts to behavioral aspects of their own and others' work and conduct. As a result, values are often seen as aspirational (+1; see FF5) rather than real, are sometimes met with cynicism (a -1 EQ response; see FF12), and fail to achieve the intended effect. And while *competencies* may provide a focus for performance review meetings and associated gradings, they may still fail to achieve the desired shifts in quality.

Fix 34:
Build Quality into *Planning!*

What's important is to understand the two main causes of the low quality of relationships and interactions that in turn generates the reaction of creating such lists!

The first cause is that in so-called "strategic planning" at Levels +1 and +2, even though most or all planned actions will need to be executed through organizational, departmental or individual 360 relationships, these key relationships are *not included* in the planning! Therefore their quality is not managed, and has to be compensated for by efforts such as values initiatives or competency frameworks. These cost extra time and money!

The second cause is that the quality of core interactions within and on behalf of the organization is at Level +1 or lower (see FF 21-30). People are not fully prepared!

The solution?

- Develop skill in using the 360 approach to planning that has been outlined in FF21, 30 and 33

- In the planning, include ways of raising interaction skills towards Level +3 (such as through internally- or externally-sourced *coaching*)

Fault 35:
Departments or Compartments?

In many organizations – and not only large ones! – there can be an absence of contact or relationship between different parts of the organization.

At first glance this may not seem important; each Team, Practice Area, Business Unit or Department feels it is carrying out its role and meeting its objectives and has no need to spend time or effort on its counterparts.

As noted in FF26, such attitudes towards peer relations are characteristic of Level +1 and below. The focus is exclusively on *tactical* rather than *strategic* thinking and consequent planning, deciding and communicating. This means that many potential benefits for the organization – such as internal hiring, cross-selling (and other business development opportunities) and creative thinking around wider opportunities for the organization – go missing.

The remedy here is again Level +3 strategic thinking and planning that includes:

- Defining or re-defining the **purpose/contribution** to be made to the organization as a whole
- Creating developmental **aims**, **metrics** and **tactics** for each of the other three 360 relationships

Fix 35:
Plan Using *360 Thinking!*

Pulling together elements of FF 12-14, 21 and 33, here are key questions for developing a Level +3 strategic plan for a department:

1. What is the desired fundamental **contribution** of the department to the organization as a whole?

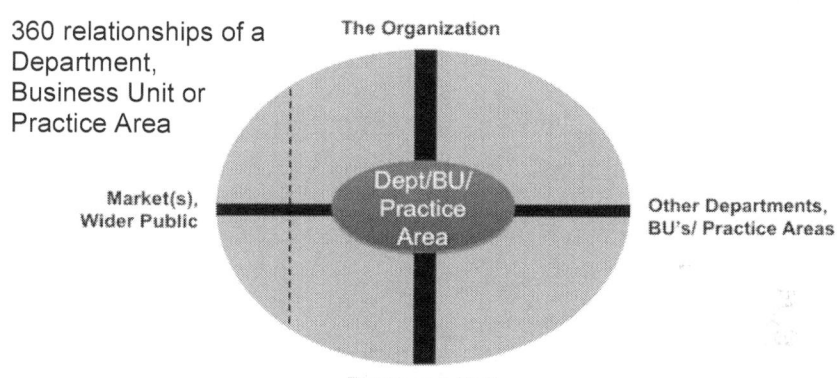

360 relationships of a Department, Business Unit or Practice Area

The Organization

Market(s), Wider Public

Dept/BU/ Practice Area

Other Departments, BU's/ Practice Areas

Teams and Staff

2. What (two or three) **aims** can we create for each of a) enhancing our external (client/market) reputation, b) creating optimal conditions for teams and individuals within the department, and c) building trust and collaboration with other departments?

3. What **metrics** and **actions** will secure each aim?

Fault 36:
Local or Global?

As businesses and other organizations have expanded internationally, the phrase *"Think Global, Act Local"* has become a popular motto in dealing with the apparent dichotomy of a global versus a local view.

At first sight it seems to make sense – an all-seeing HQ that is able to determine strategy from afar, with tactical implementation executed in the distant satellites.

This may work initially as the new structures settle; as time goes by, it may become insufficient in terms of financial leveraging of the enlarged structure.

With reference to the diagram shown in FF32, what is in effect happening is that a strategic decision on structure has resulted in the new structure itself now determining how strategy is formulated (centrally) in a way that will likely take the organizational culture as a whole down to +1 and possibly lower.

The harsh truth is that "Think Global, Act Local" comes from a well-intended Level +2 Mindset that unwittingly risks generating counter-productive (-2) divisions and the compartmentalization indicated in FF35.

Fix 36:
Cascade 360 Planning!

From a Level +3 perspective, it becomes clear that "Think Global, Act Local" has to be replaced by the less sound-bite-like but more sustainable *"Think and Act both Globally and Locally!"* What does this mean in practice? Nothing more and nothing less than:

- Creating and *integrating* 360 strategies (see FF35 and preceding) for the organization itself and each of the different parts of its structure
- Similarly creating 360 role definitions (see FF21) for all managers and staff (for managing performance)
- Instilling implicit communication skills (FF 22-30)

Suggestion: take an existing strategy that has already been developed for your organization or for your part of it. Now separate each of its elements according to the 360 relationship(s) required for implementation.

It is likely a) that much or all of the existing strategy will fit into the 360 planning structure, b) that this process will also expose aspects not yet included in the current strategy, and c) that some elements of the existing strategy are not yet connected to any relationship – and therefore risk not being actualized!

Fault 37:
Can't Attract or Retain?

From a Level 1 point of view, the reasons it can be difficult to attract or retain people are many and varied.

There can be rises and falls in the labor market, differences in how different generations expect to be treated in the workplace, or over-reliance on a sense of vocation in professions such as teaching or nursing.

And it can happen in some sectors, such as certain types of banking, that whole teams can be lured to move from one employer to another simply by differences in financial remuneration. This means that the way in which an organization presents itself initially is of key importance.

That said, the bottom line is, as the phrase goes, that *"people leave people, not organizations."* In a Level +2 culture it is increasingly understood that the major influences on attraction and retention are the *quality* of:

- The personal interactions through the hiring process and beyond as set out in FF21-30
- The strategic thinking behind them (FF31-36)

These largely determine the initial level of *engagement*.

Fix 37:
Manage *"Dead Wood"!*

One of the more subtle cultural deterrents that cause high quality people to consider moving elsewhere is the degree to which sustained poor performance is tolerated.

On a daily basis this connects directly to the quality of the Review and Confrontation interactions discussed in FF 23 and 24. If the quality of these interactions is generally poor, and especially at senior level, younger partners, associates, managers or executives may feel it is not worth committing long term as they may not be appropriately recognized and rewarded through their career.

Strong management of "dead wood" is a characteristic of Level +3 cultures – strong not in the sense of harsh or uncaring but rather in the sense of being well organized and creative. It means recognizing where there is no longer a fit and finding a solution.

Some consultancies actively propel consultants with a certain amount of experience into client organizations where the relationship continues in a different form.

Whatever the approach, defining and requiring visibly high standards for *everyone* sends important messages that in turn help attract and retain good people.

Fault 38:
Initiatives or Consultants?

A subtle source of potential demoralization, negatively impacting engagement, is the over-use of initiatives and consultants.

Here again, it's important to be clear about *why* such decisions are made, and there are significant differences connected to levels of leadership *mindset* (see FF2).

In a Level -1 mindset or culture, external consultants may be hired through a mix of fear and uncertainty, even for such crucial tasks as the creation of strategy! Senior management may feel they cannot in future be *blamed* (by shareholders or partners) for plans that were created by well-known consultants!

In reality, while the market information that consultants may bring can be valuable, there is no guarantee of high quality strategic thinking. For this reason, many costly strategic reports or draft strategies remain on the shelf.

A further significant reason that *externally-sourced* strategies may turn out to be impractical is that their implementation depends on *internal* staff who were not involved in the thinking process and, for this very reason, may not fully understand the thinking behind it and struggle to be fully engaged towards it.

Fix 38:
Coaching and Mentoring!

At Level +1, there may be a sense that the presence of external consultants is duplicating internal capability or preventing its development.

At Level +2, external consultants are confidently hired to make specific contributions towards results where the required expertise is not available internally. There may or may not be transfer of expertise through the process.

At level +3, the preference is to see first whether new challenges can be met through internal capability and, if need be, to support this by *coaching* or *mentoring* so that internal capability is strengthened for the future.

While the definitions are sometimes blurred, a mentor typically has industry experience and gives advice based on this experience, perhaps also making introductions and giving other help with networking.

A coach generates new, future-oriented thinking that results in new decisions and increased capability.

There are similar mindset differences with "initiatives," which are a Level +2 feature and can lead to "initiative fatigue." At Level +3, these are absorbed into leadership activity without such labeling.

Fault 39:
Accountable or Unaccountable?

A further challenge to employee engagement can be a sense that senior people are not held sufficiently accountable for their actions or performance.

There may be a subtler echo that accompanies this – that most if not all of us feel deep down that we have some kind of unfulfilled potential which needs articulating and making concrete in order to be realized and recognized.

To the extent that junior people feel this, they may also wish for greater accountability for themselves!

So what is it that prevents or undermines accountability?

First there is our old friend *fear*, a Level -1 emotion (see FF12) – whether fear of failure to achieve specific results or the fear of associated hostile attacks which, in many leadership positions, come with the territory.

Secondly, and also very importantly, the quality of metrics or concrete objectives may not feel appropriate or meaningful as reflections of work. This relates directly to the quality of strategic thinking and goal setting, specifically whether or not qualitative aspects are included (see FF34).

Fix 39:
Develop a *Culture of Coaching!*

So how to deal with these twin challenges of *fear* and relative *lack of meaning?* In short, how to generate confidence and a sense of purpose?

Confidence is built as a consequence of preparation, incremental achievement against meaningful goals, and recognition. The same applies for engagement!

Professionals are confident and engaged in the technical aspects of their work because they have been prepared for it, their steady achievements are relatively clear to themselves and perhaps to others, and they likely receive recognition for them, whether internally or from clients.

In matters of leadership and organizational life, they may have no preparation and may not have anticipated or wished for such a role as part of their career! To become as professional in non-technical areas as they are in technical areas requires nurturing, primarily in the topics of FF 1-38 of this book.

The embracing of coaching in these areas at senior level can lead to the evolution of a *culture of coaching* that is the hallmark of a Level +3 mindset and organization.

Fault 40:
Top-Down or Bottom-Up?

Often the question arises about whether cultural change within an organization is "top-down" – that is, initiated and driven by senior management – or "bottom-up" – that is, driven from junior levels.

The picture may also be confused where the visible *activity* associated with development, such as internal projects or programmes, are *undertaken* by junior levels yet are actively *decided on and supported* by seniors.

Here once again we are hampered by the either/or nature of the question (see FF 1-4) and the failure to take into account different levels of Mindset, Intelligence and Communication (FF 5-30). We have also seen how the level of Mindset impacts strategic thinking and learning and the effect this has on engagement (FF 31-39).

To take extreme cases, let's imagine two organizations: one with senior management at +3 mindset, middle management at +2 and junior management +1, and the other with the reverse (+3 juniors, +2 middle, +1 senior). In the first, the culture will naturally grow towards +3; in the second, junior people will leave or lack engagement and the organization will soon swing to minus levels.

Fix 40:
Reciprocal *Nourishment!*

Where cultural change is most needed – that is, in the minus levels – it is least likely to happen strategically and will need a crisis to stimulate it. Usually there will then be a structural change (of CEO or Managing Partner) to lead the establishment of +2, and quite often there will then be a further change to eliminate the negative (-2) aspects of this change in order to move towards building a +3 culture.

As with politics, if there is a real bottom-up movement for change, this will in effect be the organizational crisis that produces the structural change mentioned above and perhaps, eventually, a cultural shift.

More likely, if the movement for change is unsuccessful, those driving it will leave. And if it is "successful" there is a real risk that the old culture will simply continue with new people.

In a healthy organization there is reciprocal nourishment between higher and lower authority at each level, the lower levels providing a source of new ideas and energy, the upper levels providing meaning, direction, clear decisions, empowerment and succession planning!

Leadership Faults & Fixes

Government, Citizens and Education

The four-way relationship structure and six underlying levels of quality explored in Faults and Fixes 1-40 can also be usefully applied to Government and Citizenship.

Faults and Fixes 41-50 develop this application and the implications for Education.

Fault 41:
Information or Knowledge?

For many people, particularly those fond of technological innovation and "information technology" (IT), each year is seen as an improvement on the previous one and our progress as a species and civilization seems undeniable.

For others, things are different. They see that it is the sustained quest to improve the instruments of war that drives the creation of much technology, and that we easily become slaves to such tools rather than masters of them.

What can help us in considering relationships between Government, Citizenship and Education is to differentiate between *information, knowledge* and *understanding*.

The information that is stored and moved in ever more sophisticated ways by information technology is raw data about facts, events or people, relatively devoid of personal assimilation or interpretation.

Knowledge implies *experience*, against which data can be judged or interpreted, and can take the form of know-how. "Knowledge Management" is now a term given to the storing of know-how in professional firms so that it can be accessed and passed to others without being re-invented. Knowledge includes and transcends data/information. *Understanding* includes and transcends knowledge.

Fix 41:
Build *Understanding!*

Understanding is *practical awareness of relationship*; of how one thing or aspect connects to another; of *how the part relates to the whole*. It has to be *constructed* – not artificially but *substantially,* as the understanding of an apprentice develops under the (traditionally) seven-year guidance of the master of a craft.

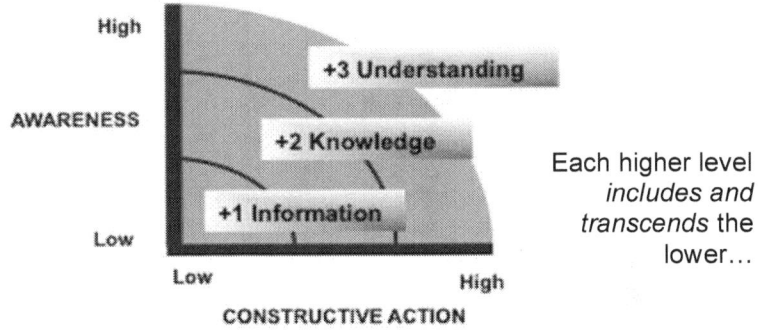

Building understanding requires bringing together the IQ component of information, the PQ aspect of knowledge and know-how and the EQ sense of inter-relationship. The master cannot simply *transfer* his or her understanding to the apprentice; the challenge is to *create an environment* in which the apprentice's understanding can *grow* through experience and intentional effort. This is important as we consider Government, Citizenship and Education.

Fault 42:
Democracy or Tyranny?

Ever since the time of Plato and Aristotle, the prevalent duality in western governmental theory and practice has been that of *tyranny* (a single ruler, whether benevolent or malevolent) and *democracy* (varying degrees of rule "by the people").

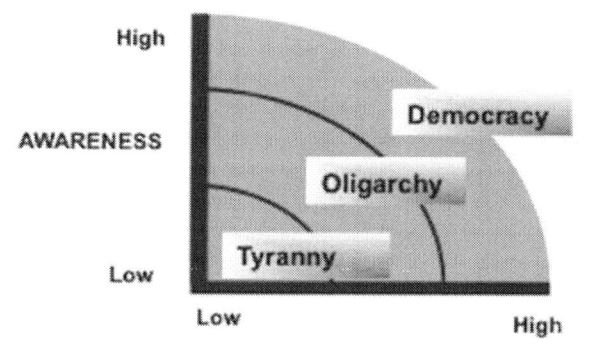

As in FF1, there is a *third,* less obvious element: **OLIGARCHY**, which sits *between* **tyranny** and **democracy**

Like Plato, constitutionalists such as James Madison have recognized the *tendency for financial inequality* within democracies – Plato in his writings favoring the less wealthy, Madison in the US constitution favoring the wealthier. Today's democracies broadly reflect these contrasting financial interests and their ideologies in the further duality of "right" and "left" within government.

Fix 42:
Recognize *Oligarchies!*

In terms of growth and decay (see FF8), *oligarchy–* meaning rule by the (wealthy, appointed) few – can be an *ascent from tyranny* (as with Magna Carta in the 13th century) or a *descent from democracy* (as some think may be happening in today's USA and Europe).

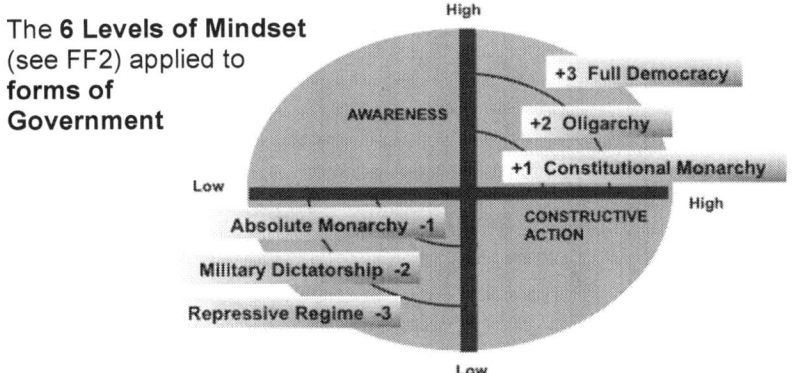

The **6 Levels of Mindset** (see FF2) applied to **forms of Government**

The six levels of Mindset apply to types of government as indicated above (using modern terminology).

Suggestion: use the Levels framework to explore other past or present forms of government, taking care (e.g. with *fascism* or *communism*) to distinguish between *theoretical* ideals and the *actual* form an ideology may have taken in practice. Note *fluctuations* (see FF11-15)!

Fault 43:
Sovereignty or Federalism?

A second duality underpinning early 21st century affairs concerns law- and policy-making functions within and between sovereign states and international bodies – and also, perhaps less obviously, between sovereign states and their component entities.

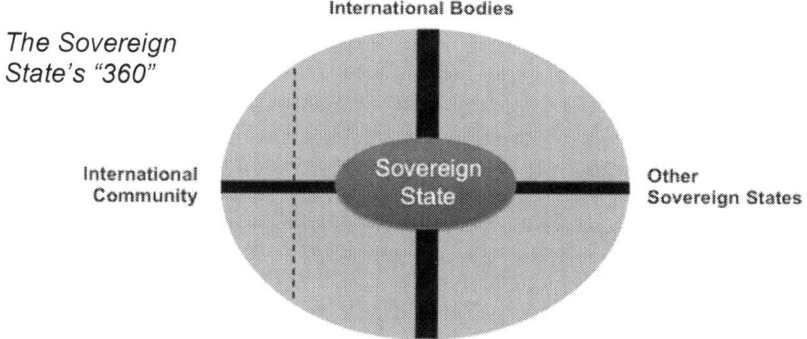

The Sovereign State's "360"

Decision-making entities within the State

The USA and Russia are sovereign states with federal structures, each occasionally experiencing secessionist movements arising from a populist sense of insufficient autonomy within internal states/republics.

In 2015-2016 the UK government experienced both a Scottish movement to leave the UK and a referendum over UK membership of the European Union. While there were financial and other issues involved, the underlying question was of sovereignty in law-making and policy.

Fix 43:
Subsidiarity!

In business, government and society alike, Level +3 decision-makers look to *raise* the level of self-determination of those in lower authority, Level +2 to *control* it, and Level +1 to *minimize* it through micro-management.

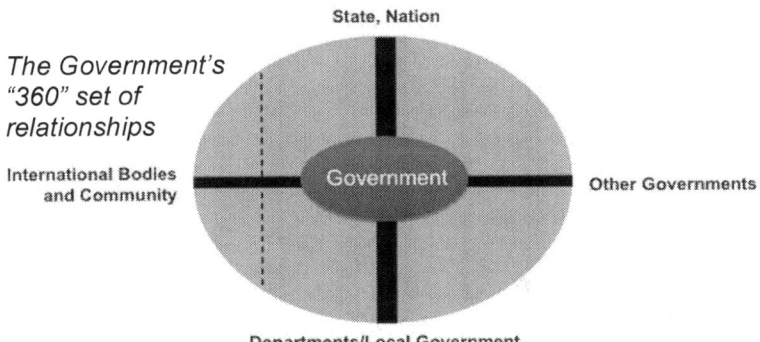

The UK government found itself sandwiched between the European Union – initially established to create a single market and seen by many as increasingly operating as a nascent federal government – and the regions of the UK. Whether or not always abiding by it, the EU is committed to the principle of *subsidiarity* – taking decision-making to the lowest level possible – as also visible in successful democracies such as Switzerland.

In the judgment of the UK electorate, subsidiarity was in effect not sufficiently observed, and they voted to leave.

Fault 44:
Constitution or Not?

A third political "either/or" question concerns whether or not to have a written constitution, as is the case in the USA and many or most countries other than the UK, whose constitution is derived from various written and unwritten sources.

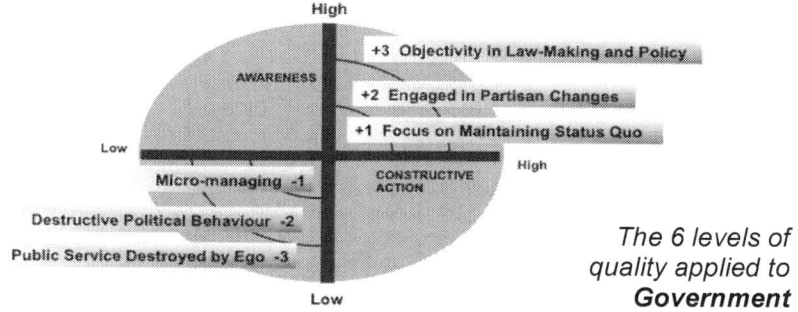

The 6 levels of quality applied to ***Government***

If we apply the framework of six levels of quality to government, this can throw light on such questions as Human Rights law. This did not emerge in the UK under partisan elected governments but, as with Workers' Rights laws, was effectively imposed by the EU in working to fulfill its ("downwards") responsibility of creating a Common Market for trade. This was law-making from above, arguably at Level +3 (though some saw it as unnecessary -1 interference) and, according to the EU, consistent with their mandate.

Fix 44:
See the *Role* of Government!

From a Level +3 perspective, the written constitution of a state corresponds to the strategy of an organization and the role definition of an individual. All can be simply built by applying the Level +3 sense of responsibility (see FF3) to their specific structure of 360 relationships.

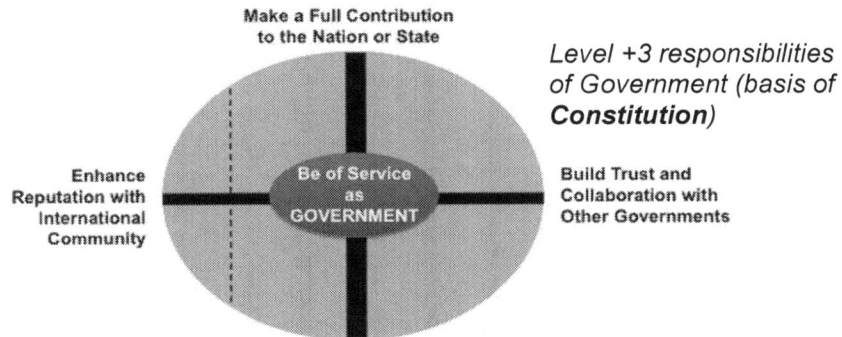

Suggestion: study the written constitution of a selected country, with reference to the following questions:

- Which of the 360 relationships are included/absent?
- To what extent are level +3 responsibilities present?
- To what extent does it give a basis for the formulation of a Level +3 government *strategy* (see FF 33-36)?

Fault 45:
Manifesto or Plan?

When prospective governing parties or officials put themselves forward for election or appointment, there is a selection process whose quality relates in some ways to the quality of organizational hiring explored in FF21. In other ways it can be very different.

Leaders with a -2 mindset of destructive dynamism (see FF2) can come into office and power initially through the democratic process, especially when a sufficient proportion of the electorate has become frustrated with the negative fluctuations of +2 (partisan) governments.

Once in power, -2 leaders may build confidence through what appear initially to be +2 partisan achievements; a danger is that their *mindset* moves the other way – towards that of -3 *destructive exclusion* – in ways that do not become evident and impactful until it is too late to avoid the development of a widespread -2 and -3 culture.

In passive cultures (-1, +1), candidates will aim to reassure voters or decision-makers of their loyalty to important aspects of the status quo, whether in articulated national interests or in the ideology of the political party they are representing. Such reassurance may be reflected in relatively inexplicit "manifestos."

Fix 45:
Make Policies *Strategic!*

In Level +2, there is more future- than past-orientation and personality may be less influential. Manifestos, as befits their definition, are *clearer* on policies – at least those on issues currently attracting attention.

Level	Mindset	Government	Citizenship	Education
6 Levels: Key Words for GOVERNMENT, CITIZENSHIP and EDUCATION				
+3	Constructive Inclusion	Objectivity in Law-Making and Policy	Creative Service to the Community	Brings Mindsets to Level +3
+2	Constructive Dynamism	Engaged in Partisan Changes	Engaged in Social/ Community Improvement	Brings Mindsets to Level +2
+1	Constructive Passivity	Focus on Maintaining Status Quo	Constructive Social Habits	Brings Mindsets to Level +1
-1	Destructive Passivity	Micro-managing	Destructive Social Habits	Results in -1 Mindsets
-2	Destructive Dynamism	Destructive Political Behavior	Self-Centred Social/ Community Involvement	Results in -2 Mindsets
-3	Destructive Exclusion	Public Service Destroyed by Ego	Destructive Influence on Community	Results in -3 Mindsets

This table outlines qualitative connections between Mindset, Government, Citizenship and Education.

A Level +3 manifesto would comprise a draft *strategy* for fulfillment of the *level +3 responsibilities* inherent in the Governmental 360 (FF44), raising public Mindset and *including current **issues*** as **tactics**.

Note: for the EU, this would mean identifying and planning for *upward, peer and external* relationships!

Fault 46:
Right or Left?

The division of governmental seating arrangements into right and left began in 1789 during the French revolution – those who supported the king sitting to the President's right, revolutionaries to the left.

The 20 Best Full Democracies	Rank	Country	System
According to the Economist magazine, in 2015 there were 20 Full Democracies in the world. Here they are shown in order of ranking, based on quality of: • Electoral process and Pluralism • Functioning of Government • Political Participation • Political Culture • Civil Liberties The System column shows whether the countries use a Proportional Representation or of First Past The Post electoral system (See FF47)	1	Norway	PR
	2	Iceland	PR
	3	Sweden	PR
	4	New Zealand	PR
	5	Denmark	PR
	6	Switzerland	PR
	7	Canada	FPTP
	8	Finland	PR
	9	Australia	PR
	10	Netherlands	PR
	11	Luxembourg	PR
	12	Ireland	PR
	13	Germany	Both
	14	Austria	PR
	15	Malta	PR
	16	UK	FPTP
	17	Spain	PR
	18	Mauritius	PR
	19	Uruguay	PR
	20	USA	FPTP

The gradual later use of these terms by political parties may have both reflected and promoted the rise of two-party systems in the USA and UK and the resulting stasis.

Fix 46:
Multi-Party Representation!

As the tables opposite and below indicate, countries with multi-party representation seem to have not only more effective democracies but also happier populations. They also tend to have greater accountability and transparency.

The 20 Happiest Countries	Rank	Country	System
According to the World Happiness Report 2015 (mainly using data from the Gallup World Poll), these are the 20 happiest countries in the world, based on:	1	Switzerland	PR
	2	Iceland	PR
	3	Denmark	PR
	4	Norway	PR
	5	Canada	FPTP
	6	Finland	PR
• GDP per Capita	7	Netherlands	PR
• Healthy life expectancy	8	Sweden	PR
• Freedom to make life choices	9	New Zealand	PR
	10	Australia	PR
• Social support	11	Israel	PR
• Generosity	12	Costa Rica	PR
• Perception of Corruption	13	Austria	PR
• Miscellaneous Other Factors	14	Mexico	PR
	15	USA	FPTP
The System column shows	16	Brazil	PR
whether the countries use a	17	Luxembourg	PR
Proportional Representation or	18	Ireland	PR
of First Past The Post	19	Belgium	PR
electoral system (See FF47)	20	UAE	N/A

Two-party systems may also reflect imperial/post-imperial "divide and rule" techniques, and be inflexible enough to prevent the voting rules from changing...

Fault 47:
PR or FPTP?

Most of the *20 Best Democracies* and *Happiest Countries* (see FF46) use an electoral system based on Proportional Representation (PR), as opposed to the First Past The Post (FPTP) winner-takes-all system used, for example, in the UK, the USA and Canada.

Two main influences seem to determine whether or not a change from FPTP to PR is voted for: a) whether or not one of the prevailing political *parties* sees it as in their *own* interests; and b) the quality of referendum *question(s)* asked. (To be sufficiently simple, referenda generally use closed, Level 1 "checking" questions – see FF4.)

Mixed Member PR (MMP) was adopted in New Zealand in 1996 following referenda in 1992 and 1993 driven by election campaign promises. In the first, voters were asked a) whether or not the current system should be changed, and b) if so, which of four alternative systems would be preferable (thus driving information about types of PR). In the second, they were asked to choose FPTP or MMP.

By contrast, in the UK 2011 referendum brought as a Tory party concession to the Liberal Democrats in forming a coalition, the single (Level -1) question was whether or not to change the current FPTP system to the "Alternative Vote" (not a PR system). The vote was negative and the party obligation thus honored, whether or not fully!

Fix 47:
Put *Tactics* into Context!

We make decisions based on information, knowledge or understanding (see FF41) in response to corresponding levels of question (see FF4).

In the UK referenda of 2011 (just mentioned) and 2016 (to remain in or leave the EU), there was little or no effort to create knowledge or understanding around the options, and such information as was given was advanced largely to support campaign arguments, little of it verifiable.

How can voters become better equipped to decide? Let's consider how a judge in a court case makes decisions!

The *external threefoldness* of two lawyers arguing before a judge is mirrored by an *internal threefoldness* in the judge's IQ, where the two *subjective* arguments must be assessed and resolved *relatively objectively*. In a further threefoldness, the judge sits *above* the "lower" *arguments* and *below* the "higher" *laws* that must be invoked and *interpreted* in the particular case. It's all at Level +3!

To reach this kind of quality, voters need a government that is able to formulate and communicate *strategy* (see FF33), so that there is something "higher" than tactics. This could raise mindset levels and transcend the Level +1 tactical dualities that intentionally or unintentionally serve to drain attention and preserve the status quo.

Fault 48:
Race or Gender?

When somebody new arrives, as with hiring in a business, they need to be given the chance to be part of it, to join in. The leadership responsibility (felt and acted upon at Level +3) is to create the environment where this happens.

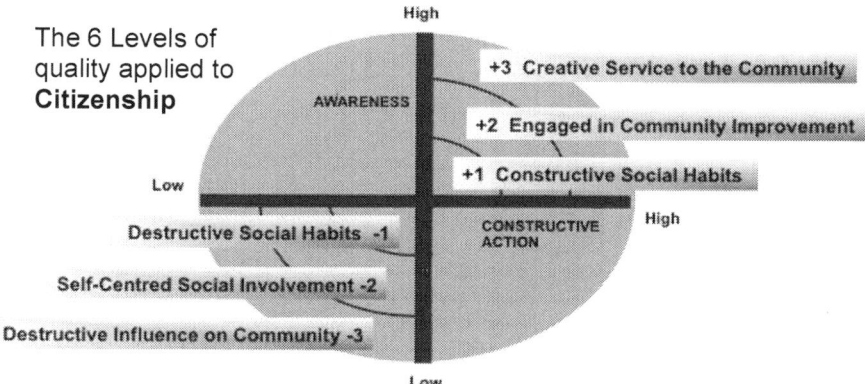

Whether unexpected immigrants or unwanted children, how or why they arrived is not the point. That comes earlier, as part of (lack of) strategy! If they are now here, they need the opportunity to get involved constructively, whether at Level +1, +2 or +3 (see above).

Creating such an environment cannot be left to chance! If it is, then the risk of negative social impact is created. This surely applies to all "minorities" – that is, people who feel they are not yet acknowledged and included!

Fix 48:
Constructive Inclusion!

Diversity needs to be welcomed and embraced openly and constructively, so that unity of purpose can be created and re-created. If this leadership responsibility is not met, it may be replaced by "political correctness" (see FF68).

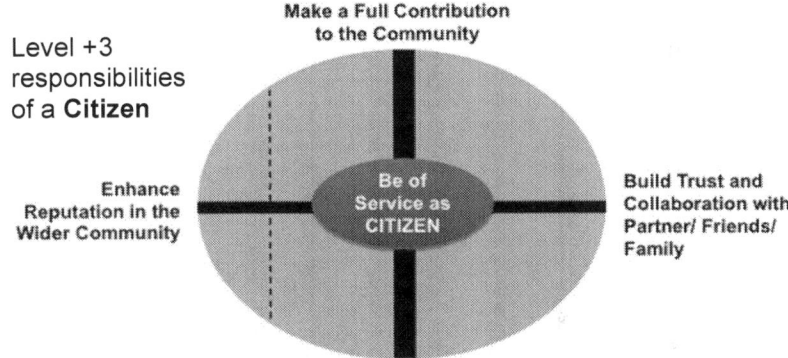

Level +3 responsibilities of a **Citizen**

Make a Full Contribution to the Community

Enhance Reputation in the Wider Community

Be of Service as CITIZEN

Build Trust and Collaboration with Partner/ Friends/ Family

Create and sustain the physical, mental and emotional Environment in which children and junior citizens contribute fully and fulfil their potential

As modern citizens we may be fortunate enough to be able to exercise choice in the community or communities we wish to join and become part of. To the extent that this is so, we may find it easier to make our contribution and to fulfill in diverse ways the responsibilities of citizenship.

A core focus of education is surely to foster this sense of belonging and contribution, alongside the growth of the different types of intelligence (see FF 11-20).

Fault 49:
Big Business & Big Government?

Business and Government have come to influence and sometimes control areas that seem to stand outside the obvious remits of providing goods and services and of making laws. These include scientific research, education, the media, journalism and many more.

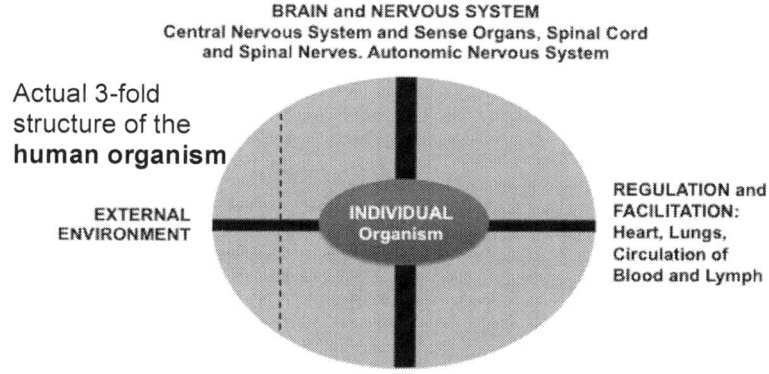

Actual 3-fold structure of the **human organism**

BRAIN and NERVOUS SYSTEM
Central Nervous System and Sense Organs, Spinal Cord and Spinal Nerves. Autonomic Nervous System

EXTERNAL ENVIRONMENT

INDIVIDUAL Organism

REGULATION and FACILITATION: Heart, Lungs, Circulation of Blood and Lymph

METABOLISM and MOVEMENT
Digestive Tract, Abdominal Organs, Limbs and Movement System

It is clear to many people that this is far from ideal. To see what might work better, we can first examine the structure of a healthy human organism (see diagram above). This has two sets of very different systems – a) the brain and nervous system and b) the metabolic and moving systems – that are brought into relationship and mutual exchange through the regulating and facilitating functions of the heart, lungs and respiratory and circulatory systems.

Fix 49:
Threefold Social Structure!

We've seen that modern organizations typically reflect Level 1 and Level 2 Mindsets (see FF 21-40). How can the *structure* of *society* evolve to reflect the structure of *healthy* humans with **Level +3 mindsets**? To see this, we'll compare social structure with the diagram opposite.

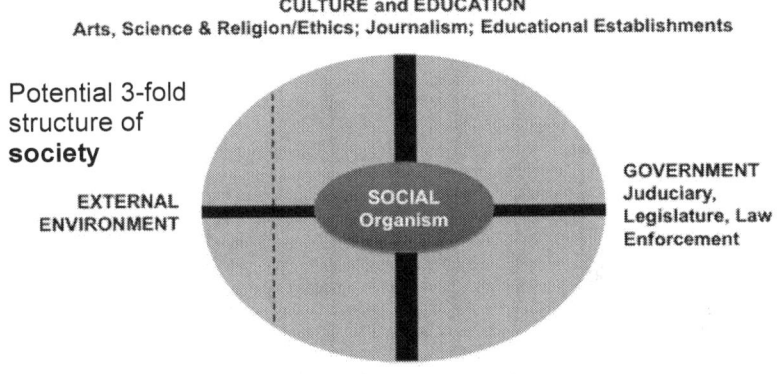

If we take away Education and, with it, Culture from the direct control of Government, a threefold structure can emerge paralleling that of an individual. The government plays a regulating and facilitative role similar to that of corresponding organs and systems in the body.

How can this evolve? Since structure follows strategy and strategy follows culture, it will likely require a Level +3 government to create a strategy for a healthy society!

Fault 50:
Schools or Academies?

A common characteristic of Level -1 Government is micro-managing (see FF45, table), which is connected to the Level 1 tendencies to fail to empower (see FF22) and to try to impose *cultural* growth through *structural* changes (see FF8 and FF32).

A clear example illustrating the coming together of micro-management, failure to empower and such structural changes is the imposition by a UK Education Minister in 2015 of lists of *specific words* that all 11-year-olds in the UK should know and be able to spell correctly. (The Minister herself publicly misspelt one of them!)

While no doubt well intended, such interference can only serve to further undermine the authority and morale of the teaching profession and to lead commentators to question whether government should be involved in education at all (or indeed anything other than defence, foreign affairs and law-making).

What is missing is clarity around the broad purpose and aims of education, which it can then be left to experts in the field to decide how to meet. And why not include a wider variety of educational experts in formulating such purpose and aims, empowering them and recognizing and expanding their leadership!

Fix 50:
Think *"Higher"!*

In Government, Citizenship and Education, as well as in other types of organizations and our own mindsets, there is a tendency to think, decide and communicate at a *tactical* level (Level +1) of awareness and action, without articulating broader purpose and intent (see FF 12-14).

The phrase "Events, dear boy, events!" – attributed to British Prime Minister Harold MacMillan on being asked what was most likely to blow governments off course – is a good example of the prevalence of *tactics without strategy*. Where there is complete thinking, events are at a tactical level and can be accommodated by adjusting the corresponding aims, metrics and actions. Without a broad strategy, all we can do is *react* to events!

Suggestion: with reference to the diagrams in FF49, imagine that you have been asked to create a Government strategy based on a new formulation of the Purpose of Government: *to regulate and facilitate the smooth functioning of culture and education, on the one hand, and the provision of goods and services, on the other.*

What aims and metrics can you invent for the fulfillment of this new Purpose? What strategic questions would need to be addressed? What resistance could be anticipated? How could industrial strikes be made unnecessary?

Leadership Faults & Fixes

Measuring and Transforming Leadership

The four-way relationship structure and six underlying levels of quality explored in FF 1-50 together constitute a framework that uses emotional intelligence to measure and develop leadership in all contexts from the psychological to the governmental.

In FF 51-60 we'll explore its application across numerous contexts as a rapid and effective assessment or self-assessment tool that connects directly to developmental planning and transformation.

Fault 51:
Extravert or Introvert?

Psychometrics and similar analytics are a Level +1 tool comprising *closed* or *multiple-choice* questions, with responses interpreted (often by computer) to determine "preferences" between selected polarities.

They can be useful in creating an initial focus on aspects of mindset. Downsides include restrictive polarizations, analysis without development, lack of direct connection or relevance to leadership or culture, avoidance of the whole question of *consciousness*, and loss of time to arguments on the validity of the analytical system itself.

This means that time and energy for self-development can be lost or subverted, sometimes with the illusion that it has actually been addressed. (In the minus levels of mindset there is no interest in such analysis.)

Level +2 psychometrics are broadly those used to help with decision-making, such as in hiring.

Level +3 psychological metrics are *integrated with development aims* (see FF 13-14). They require Level +3 points of reference so that aims can emerge. Such reference points for development are set out in FF 1-20.

Fix 51:
Measure *Mindset!*

Suggestion: For an initial sense of what's possible here, try the following steps with reference to FF 1-20 and to the specific FF indicated in the left-hand column below.

Self-Assessing Center of Gravity of Mindset and Intelligence				
FF Ref	Contexts	Current Level	Desired Level	Opportunities to Develop
11	**Mindset**			
13, 16	**IQ**			
12, 15	**EQ**			
14, 17	**PQ**			
YOUR AVERAGE:				

Working alone or with the help of a coach:
- Make a self-assessment of the *center of gravity* of your overall mindset and of each type of intelligence, noting current and desired levels as indicated above
- Also note the main ways in which your IQ, EQ, PQ and overall mindset oscillate or fluctuate
- If possible, have a partner or close colleague check and comment on your self-assessment
- Use the data generated to create development aims, metrics and actions as shown in FF 13-14 (this, and only this, is the purpose of analysis at level +3!)

Fault 52:
360 or Engagement Surveys?

As a general rule, organizations using *anonymous* 360 or engagement surveys are, in terms of the framework set out in this book, level +1 organizations looking to "do the right thing" to *manage* performance or culture.

There may be some quick wins caused by the raising of awareness through the process. Generally these are limited and do not bring the culture to level +2, because the *leadership* within 360 relationships that determines employee engagement is not sufficiently skilled.

In particular, 360 surveys can backfire because the skills of both giving and receiving feedback are undeveloped, to the extent that a reviewee may vow to "find out who wrote that" and "get even!"

At Level +2, 360 surveys include names of respondents and are consciously intended to help raised the quality of relationships and culture. Constructive dialogues may follow the analysis, perhaps with external facilitation.

At level +3, the seeking and offering of feedback is *naturally* included in the conduct and management of relationships and can be used to update 360 planning.

Fix 52:
Measure *Communication!*

Suggestion: To start measuring your communication, try the following steps with reference to the table in FF30 and to the more detailed FF indicated in the left-hand column below:

FF	Interactions (see table FF30)	Current Level	Desired Level	Opportunities to Develop
	Self-Assessing Center of Gravity of Communication			
21	Defining Roles			
22	Delegating			
23	Reviewing			
24	Reprimanding			
25	Complaining			
26	Clients Meetings			
27	Team Meetings			
28	Brainstorming			
29	Negotiating			
YOUR AVERAGE:				

- Self-assess your *center of gravity* in each interaction noting current and desired levels and opportunities
- Use the data generated to create development aims, metrics and actions (see FF 13-14) – either working alone or with a colleague, partner, leader or coach
- Work through the plan and then review and renew it!

Fault 53:
Coercive or Affiliative?

Level +1 leadership assessment tools include *styles*. One popular set comprises *coercive, affiliative, democratic, pace-setting, visionary* and *coaching*. While at first sight seeming closer to realities of leadership, such tools can suffer from similar limitations to those of FF 51 and 52.

	A *Complete (+3), Strategic* Delegation Meeting	Corresponding Leadership "Styles"
1	Welcome and recognition	Affiliative
2	Overview of bigger picture	Visionary
3	Short term goal/requirement	Visionary/ Pacesetting
4	Checking of readiness to act	Visionary/ Pacesetting
5	Recognition of positive attitude	Affiliative
6	Asking for ideas to meet the goal	Democratic
7	Recognition of quality of ideas	Affiliative
8	Agreement on concrete follow-up	Pacesetting
9	Fulfillment of follow-up	Pacesetting
Note: the **Coaching** Style includes *all* the above elements; the **Coercive** style includes *only* elements 6 and 8, both *dictated*.		

To connect such "styles" realistically and accurately to leadership interactions, such as the Delegation meeting as illustrated above, requires level +2 know-how. At a deeper level (+3), it is understood that the elements of interaction depend on *attitude*, which depends on the leader's sense of *responsibility*. So why not measure responsibility!

Fix 53:
Measure *Responsibility!*

Research on Emotional Intelligence (EQ) indicates that *self*-assessment in both psychometrics and 360 surveys can routinely give similar, even more stringent results than those involving others' feedback. Hence the self-assessment approaches suggested in FF 51 and 52.

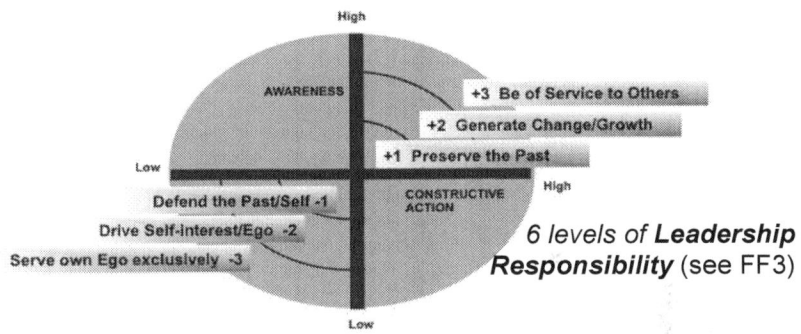

*6 levels of **Leadership Responsibility** (see FF3)*

Further suggestion: As with FF51 and FF52, assess your own level of responsibility based on the diagram above (see FF3), taking care to differentiate between actual and aspirational (see FF5). It can be useful to note if, how and when your sense of responsibility fluctuates, and to check your thoughts on this with a colleague or coach.

What is the *center of gravity* of your responsibility? (Note this for your use in FF58!).

Fault 54:
Off-sites or Jollies?

There are many potential benefits of off-site activities for teams, management groups and whole departments. They can foster creative and constructive exchanges and positively impact collaboration in the period that follows.

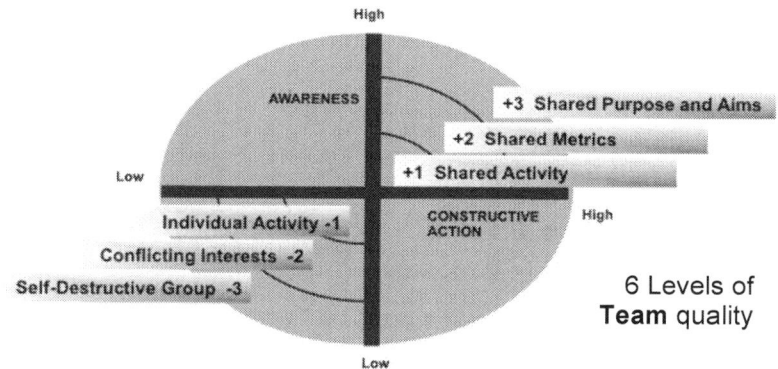

How to make the most of such events and the significant investment implied (travel, venue, opportunity costs)?

A *strategic* approach means that all such gatherings are seen as opportunities to renew or raise levels of both individual and collective *mindsets* (see FF27). Planning should therefore itself be *strategic* (see FF33-40), mostly likely including quality time for creative interactions as discussed in FF 28 and 29.

Fix 54:
Measure *Teams & Organization!*

Using the 6 Levels can be a useful and quick way to start preparing for team, departmental and organizational off-sites. This can clarify the *contribution* (purpose/mission) of the meeting from which aims and metrics can emerge.

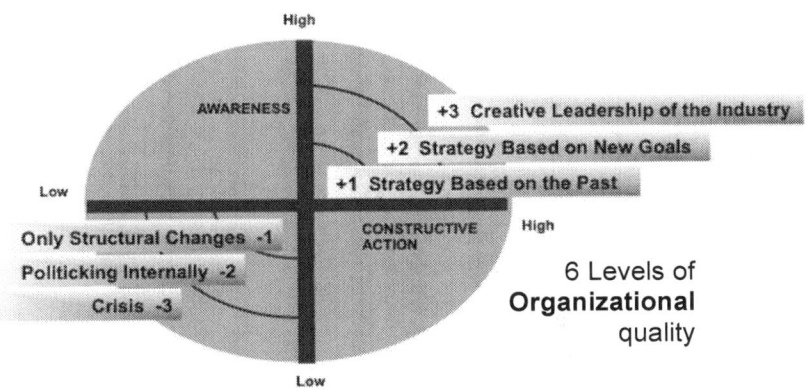

In using the 6 Levels, it's important to remember that each higher level *includes and transcends* the level below it. For example, at Level +2 in the Team view opposite, the team members are working towards shared metrics, as perhaps in a sales team. If the team is at Level +3, then "shared metrics" means that each team member *knows* the others' metrics, which may be different from their own, and can therefore help with ideas for achieving them. (Note: if post-event feedback is based on what people *liked or disliked*, this indicates Level 1; see FF12).

131

Fault 55:
Giver or Receiver?

While we may be familiar with John F. Kennedy's dictum "Ask not what your country can do for you; ask what you can do for your country," what we *can* actually do, other than pay taxes, may not be so obvious.

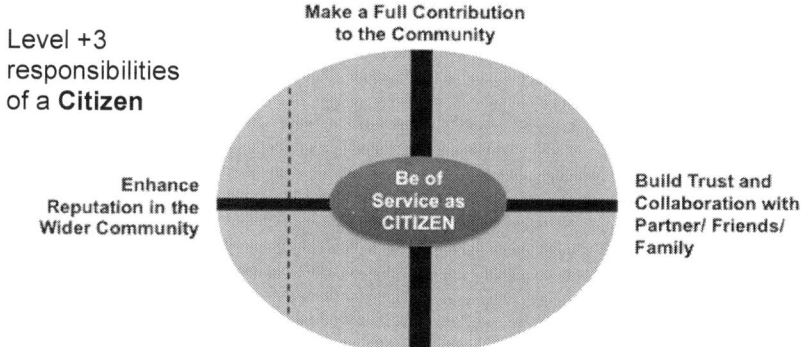

Level +3
responsibilities
of a **Citizen**

Make a Full Contribution
to the Community

Enhance
Reputation in the
Wider Community

Be of
Service as
CITIZEN

Build Trust and
Collaboration with
Partner/ Friends/
Family

Create and sustain the physical, mental and emotional Environment
in which children and junior citizens contribute fully and fulfil their potential

In our local communities there are many who need help. At the same time we need to think through what help is really needed – to provide a hungry person with fish, or to teach them how to catch their own?

And if we wish to be of service in some way, it may be useful that, as in air travel when we are advised to fasten our own oxygen masks before helping someone else, we need to make sure that our own house is in order first!

Fix 55:
Measure *your Citizenship!*

As with other contexts, there is an opportunity to be creative and strategic rather than passive or reactive. Again, it can help to use the 360-relationship framework as a starting point for developing intent and activity (see opposite).

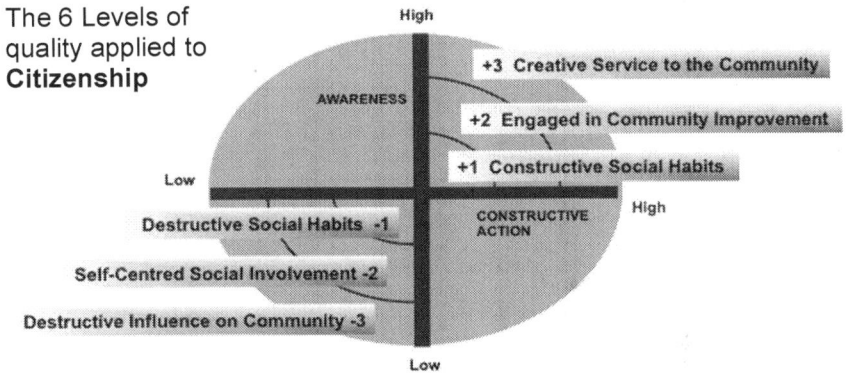

The 6 Levels of quality applied to **Citizenship**

- High
- AWARENESS
- Low
- +3 Creative Service to the Community
- +2 Engaged in Community Improvement
- +1 Constructive Social Habits
- CONSTRUCTIVE ACTION
- High
- Destructive Social Habits -1
- Self-Centred Social Involvement -2
- Destructive Influence on Community -3
- Low

Since there may be no immediate guidance or request for community involvement around us, being strategic and intentional in this way may be the only way of starting.

Applying the 6 levels as shown above can be a quick way to test the quality of our involvement. What do we already give and receive? What more can we give? When we give more – not of money but of ourselves – what does that give *us?* There may be new meaning to be found...

Fault 56:
Vote or Not Bother?

How to decide whether to vote or not? And if voting, how to decide which *way* to vote?

Depending on the country or region and on the quality of the voting system, there may or not seem to be much incentive to go to the polling station to vote. What difference will it make?

And when voting, many of us vote out of habit – whether our own habit that we have developed over a period, or simply one that we have inherited or copied.

As we started to explore in FF 43-50, it may be that we are living at a time when the role of government itself is becoming less certain than it was, and when new ideas and energy are needed to invigorate and refresh public life. Now, does the idea of contributing to *that* appeal?

With live broadcasts of government proceedings and a certain amount of increased transparency emerging, the workings of public life are becoming more accessible to those outside it and the ways of influencing it potentially more varied and informed.

Why not pick a particular area or two in which to become active? Take part in public gatherings or question-and-answer TV shows? Making your voice heard...!

Fix 56:
Measure *your Government!*

For those who find themselves irritated with or bored by the pace, focus or effectiveness of local or national government, perhaps there are opportunities to explore and eventually recommend new approaches that will make it all more interesting!

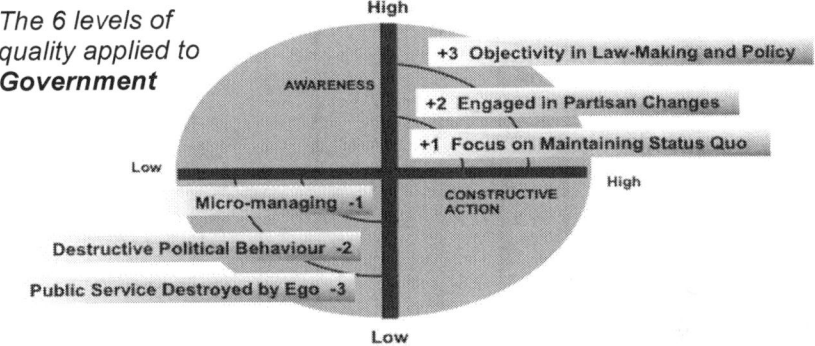

The 6 levels of quality applied to **Government**

Suggestion: take a moment to assess your government using the 6 levels (above) and also referring to the Level +3 responsibilities shown in FF44, focusing on the following questions:

- What is the Government's view of its own Purpose?
- What are its articulated *aims* in foreign relations?
- To what extent does it actively/creatively *empower*, as opposed to *micro-manage?*

Fault 57:
Fragmented Measurement?

As we have seen in FF 51-56, the common ways of measuring the quality of leadership in contexts such as mindset, intelligence, communication, organization and government are many and varied and don't join up. The framework set out in this book enables joined up (self-) assessment and reveals links between the contexts.

	Key words for INDIVIDUAL RESPONSIBILITY and each of the INNER CONTEXTS				
Level	**Context 1** Individual Responsibility	**Context 2** Mindset	**Context 3** Intellectual Intelligence (IQ)	**Context 4** Emotional Intelligence (EQ)	**Context 5** Physical Intelligence (PQ)
+3	Be of Service	Constructive Inclusion	Objective Thought	Unconditional Feelings	Full Vitality, Presence
+2	Generate Change/Growth	Constructive Dynamism	Constructive Thought	Constructive Passions	Constructive Appetites
+1	Preserve the Past	Constructive Passivity	Positive Associations	Likes; Positive Reactions	Positive Tensions
-1	Defend the Past/ Self	Destructive Passivity	Negative Associations	Dislikes; Negative Reactions	Negative Tensions
-2	Drive Self- Interest/ Ego	Destructive Dynamism	Destructive Thoughts	Destructive Passions	Destructive Appetites
-3	Serve Own Ego Exclusively	Destructive Exclusion	Fragmented Thoughts	Emotional Prison	Impaired or Ruined Vitality

The table *above* shows key words for the six levels of individual responsibility together with those of the *inner* contexts of Mindset, IQ, EQ and PQ as elaborated in FF 1-20. The table opposite again shows levels of individual responsibility, this time alongside the *outer* contexts, as elaborated in FF 31-50.

Fix 57:
Joined-Up **Measurement!**

This framework of nine contexts of leadership allows (self-) assessment of the full spectrum of leadership contexts. It can be tailored by omitting less relevant or adding in further contexts (such as *team)*, so that a single score can emerge (see FF58). This EQ-based tool can be applied to a wide range of topics (such as in FF 61-70).

	Key words for INDIVIDUAL RESPONSIBILITY and each of the OUTER CONTEXTS				
	Context 1	**Context 6**	**Context 7**	**Context 8**	**Context 9**
Level	*Individual Responsibility*	**Depts, BU's, PA's**	**Organization**	**Citizenship**	**Government**
+3	*Be of Service*	Joint Development of Culture	Creative L'ship of Industry	Creative Service to the Community	Objectivity in Law-Making and Policy
+2	*Generate Change/ Growth*	Collaboration with other Depts, BU's, PA's	Strategy based on New Goals	Engaged in Community Improvement	Engaged in Partisan Changes
+1	*Preserve the Past*	Routine Business & Procedures	Strategy based on Past	Constructive Social Habits	Focus on Maintaining Status Quo
-1	*Defend the Past/ Self*	Distance from Other Depts, BU's, PA's	Only Structural Changes	Destructive Social Habits	Micro-managing
-2	*Drive Self-Interest/ Ego*	Silo Mentality; Unco-ordinated Business Dev	Politicking Internally	Self-Centred Social/Community Involvement	Destructive Political Behaviour
-3	Serve Own Ego Exclusively	Mutual Undermining of Effectiveness	Crisis	Destructive Influence on Community	Public Service Destroyed by Ego

Additional ways of tailoring the framework include:
- Tailoring and expanding the *wording* of the 6 Levels
- Adding 6 to all scores so that all are positive (3 to 9)
- Further sub-dividing each Level to a scale of 10, so that the full range of gradations runs from 30 to 99

Fault 58:
Assessment or Development?

Why do we assess and self-assess?

For some, assessment is justifiable and valid for its own sake. "It's x this year; let's see if it gets to $x+5$ next year." The main criterion is an intellectual one of information that has the appearance of being objective, as if analyzing the physical characteristics of a piece of wood.

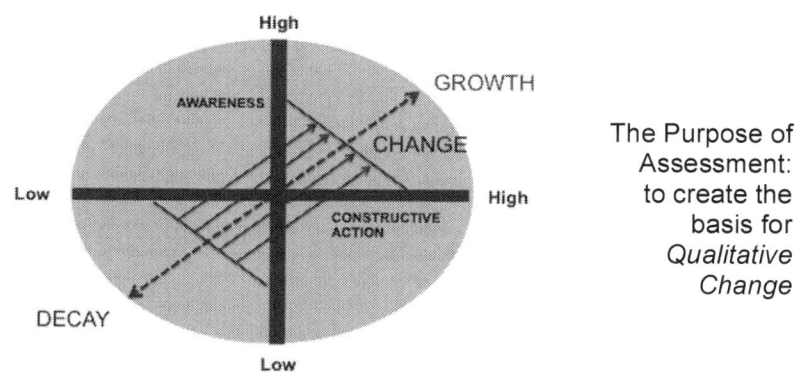

The Purpose of Assessment: to create the basis for *Qualitative Change*

The approach presented here is different because the purpose is to create the basis for *qualitative change* through, initially, the formulation of development *aims*. For this it is necessary to tap into *understanding* rather than simply *information* (see FF41).

This approach to assessment uses EQ rather than IQ.

Fix 58:
Plan for *Transformation!*

As indicated in FF57, there are ways to tailor the wording and develop detailed categorizations for each context. Generally this is unnecessary, as the detail will emerge in the planning process. All that's needed initially is to decide which contexts to assess and work on.

| | Measuring Leadership | | | |
See FF	Contexts	Current Level	Desired Level	Opportunities to Develop
51	Mindset			
52	Communication			
53	Responsibility			
54	Team			
59	Coaching			
31	Department			
54	Organization			
55	Citizenship			
56	Government			
YOUR SCORE:				

The selection of contexts above includes Citizenship and Government. Additionally or alternatively, one could include each type of intelligence separately, as in FF51.

What's important is to *use* the fundamental levels in each context as a stimulus for the creation of *intent* (see FF12).

139

Fault 59:
Tomorrow or Next Month?

The quality of coaching and self-coaching will determine the quality of transformation. Its subject matter spans the topics of FF 1-40.

Coaching at its best is a form of Level +3 leadership. That said, we need to recognize that labeling someone a *coach* does not mean that they behave as a +3 leader.

In the destructive levels of leadership mindset (-2 and -3), the frustrations of the so-called "coach" – if there is one – produce approaches to altering others' behavior that can become coercive and may use violent language. This is visible in the styles of some sports "coaches."

In a Level -1 culture, coaching is rare. If used, it is seen as a remedial device and may become viewed as a sign of weakness in performance. In Level +1, the focus is simply on helping the coachee to follow *precedent* accurately.

In Level +2, coaching is seen as a particular type of interaction ("now I'm going to coach you") to help the coachee improve. It may be confined to technical areas, and include instruction. Whatever its focus, the starting point at this Level is *the coach's own "filter* (see FF9).

There's rarely an easy or "right" time to start coaching…

Fix 59:
Coaching – *Now!*

In Level +3 leadership, coaching becomes a style that permeates *all* leadership interactions and develops the culture positively and continuously from within.

The ways in which the coaching style appears in each of the key leadership interactions are set out in FF 21-30. At the heart is that *all begins from the coachee's "filter."*

Coaching and
Self-Coaching –
the *habit* of
Growth

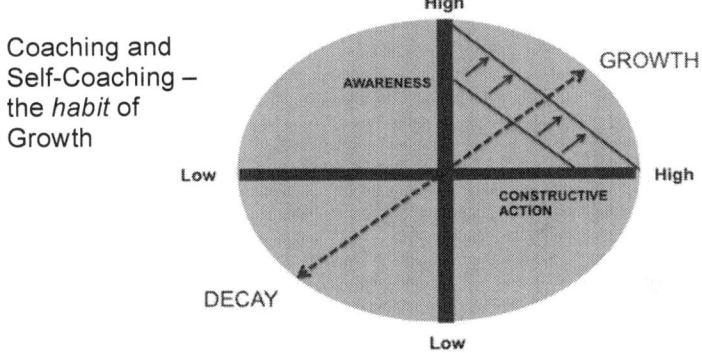

Coaching is the optimal style for intentionally and consciously providing *good leadership* (see FF 2-3). At Level +3 the focus is always the *coachee's* "filter" and *understanding.* Expert coaching requires Level +3 EQ, IQ and PQ (see FF11). Through it, continuous learning generates the *habit* of growth... starting NOW!

Fault 60:
Coaching or Self-Coaching?

In organic life, most things seem to eat something else, or to be food for something else, or both.

We are more or less aware of what we eat, and perhaps to some extent of the effect our selected food has on us. We may also sense that the air we breathe and the impressions we receive through our sense organs are a kind of food.

What's harder to get a feel for is: for whom or what are *we ourselves* food? What do we nourish?

First, we provide food for everyone we meet, since we are included in the impressions *they* receive through *their* sense organs. To the extent that they process this "food," we become part of their "digested" experience.

Secondly, we are food for *ourselves*! Perhaps uniquely among sentient beings, we have the possibility of self-observation. For many people, this is done only through hindsight and memory, with relatively few moments of immediate self-awareness, perhaps stimulated by crisis.

For others, it is possible to bring *oneself* into question – thoughts, emotions, physical appetites, communication and overall impact on others – in a way that creates inner openness, flexibility and self-knowledge.

Fix 60:
Transcend Duality!

Coaching and, to the extent that we become able to do it, self-coaching, are ways through which we can develop our self-knowledge and, through that, our inner and outer awareness.

Good coaching also goes further; it facilitates our creative decision-making in contexts such as those shown in FF58.

FF 1-59 of this book set out a framework for coaching and self-coaching. What is the ultimate goal?

Beyond the benefits of ideas and insights that can help address business and other public and private situations, there is a potentially deeper and still more meaningful change that awaits us: the experience of *transcending duality.*

As the "Faults and Fixes" set out within the book reveal, we live largely in a world of dualities – this and that, good and bad, more or less, right or left – and this tends to determine and limit the quality of our experience.

We *can* transcend duality and, as the remainder of the book indicates, we *need* to!

Leadership Faults & Fixes

The Future of Leadership, Culture and Humanity

In this concluding set of "Faults and Fixes," we'll apply the 4-way relationships and 6 Levels of Awareness and Action framework to a range of further dualities, dichotomies and dilemmas that feature in current human experience.

And then: How to *"press the refresh button"?*

Fault 61:
Progress or Regress?

How to assess whether our species is progressing, regressing or standing still? Not easy, since (leaving aside religious convictions for now) *we don't know the purpose of humanity* and therefore we have no measureable *strategy* for fulfilling it! We do not and currently cannot think or feel at that level.

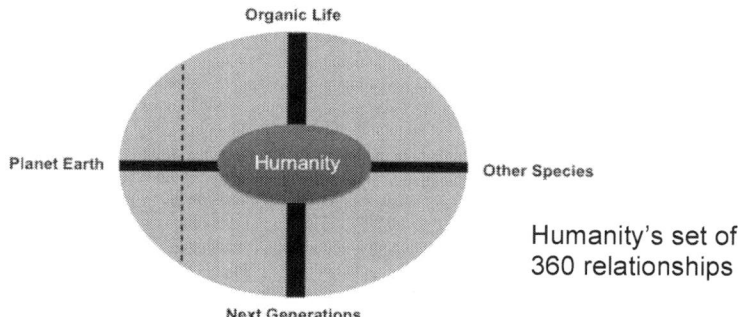

Humanity's set of
360 relationships

Applying the 360-relationship model from FF1, we can place Organic Life on Earth above us (it is the most immediate "creator" of our environment and even contains the remains of our forbears!). "Below" us are the future generations whose environment we are accidentally or intentionally creating, with other species as our "peers." The combined quality of these relationships surely impacts our "mother" Earth!

Fix 61:
See *Repetition!*

If we take the six levels of quality shown in FF57 as a guide – particularly the *inner* contexts – we can see that throughout human history there have been conscious efforts and influences to raise levels and fluctuating highs and lows in terms of prevailing quality.

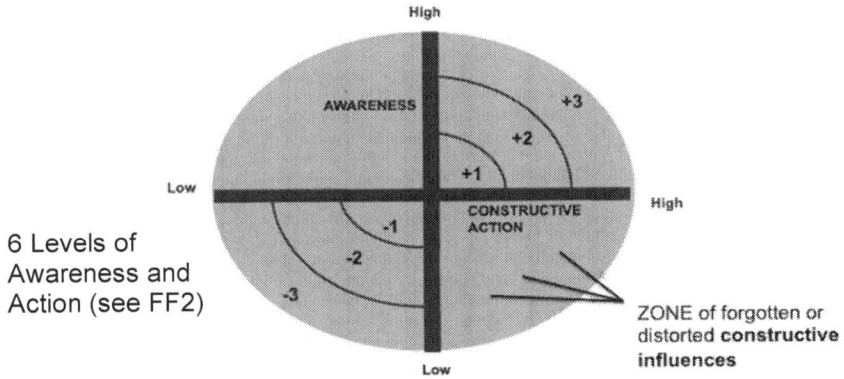

6 Levels of
Awareness and
Action (see FF2)

The lower right quadrant of the Levels diagram is the zone of *past constructive influences that are still acted upon,* where the original purpose and intent are forgotten or distorted. A simple example is our seven-day week! We continue using it, unaware of and largely uninterested in who originated it, where, when and for what reason(s). (Do we assume they were "inferior" to us...?)

Fault 62:
War or Peace?

We saw in FF61 that the lower right quadrant of the 6 Levels framework is the zone of influences that retain a constructive impact even though the original purpose and intent are forgotten or distorted.

What about the *upper left* quadrant?

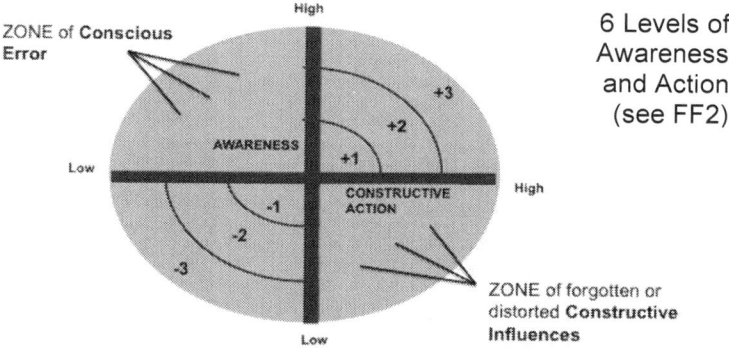

Here there is *high awareness* with *destructive action*. In interpreting this, we have to be careful because much destructive action (-2) is caused by *lack* of awareness, while the intentional demolition, say, of one building in order to replace it by another is a -2 action *transformed* under a +2 or +3 mindset.

The top left quadrant is the zone of *conscious error*.

Fix 62:
See, Feel and Admit *Error!*

The first time we make a mistake we might not be to blame. When we knowingly make it again and again, understanding its negative consequences, this is the kind of error characteristic of the top left quadrant.

In an individual this may correspond broadly to "sin" (a word derived through translation from the Greek for "mistake") and can be particularly harmful when it concerns one of the so-called "seven deadly" sins.

In collective life it corresponds most notably to our constantly recurring *wars*, waged by "leaders" with negative mindsets who reduce the focus of attention to slaughter and "victory." This sickness seems guaranteed well into the future by the twin perceived needs of self-centeredly controlling natural resources (oil, gas, water) and sustaining the lucrative armaments industry.

The US Declaration of Independence echoed Greek philosopher Epicurus in emphasizing "the pursuit of happiness," regrettably stopping short of including his *definition* of happiness, which was: *"peace of mind"!*

FF 24-28 provide the approaches and steps needed for addressing and eliminating *repeated errors*. First, there must simply be a wish to do so!

Fault 63:
Debt and Credit?

For millennia, money has been the medium used by successive empires and civilizations to facilitate the production and exchange of goods and services both within and between communities. It has been referred to as the "blood" of society as it enables resources to flow to the desired destinations.

At the same time, the purchasing power of money, which is based on an explicit or tacit assumption of its value, has also in effect made it into *a commodity itself* that can be "bought" (for example in foreign exchange) or "rented" (in the sense that interest, for example, can be seen as a form of rent). Hence there are sophisticated markets in buying and selling debt and other instruments.

The fractional reserve banking system used in many countries means that money and debt are created simultaneously. This can allow many new things to become possible (+2) and at the same time enables abuses (-2) depending on controlling mindsets.

Again we can use the 6 levels framework as a way of connecting the use of money to *responsibility* (see diagram opposite, based on that of FF2).

Fix 63:
Review the *Purpose* of Money!

Greek philosophy has influenced much over the last 2,500 years, and it's worth noting that the types of government shown in FF41 (oligarchy, democracy and tyranny) are only numbers three, four and five respectively in Plato's total of five categories.

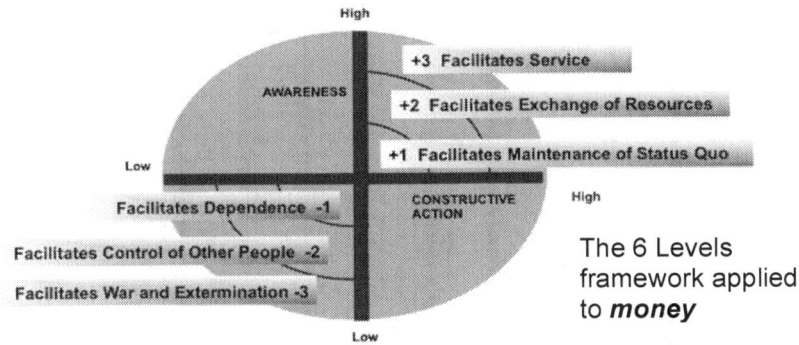

The 6 Levels framework applied to *money*

His top two, *aristocracy* and *timocracy*, differ in the their approach to spiritual and material wealth. His highly evolved "aristocrats" have no personal possessions, to avoid potential corruption in their decision-making for the benefit of others, while his less evolved "timocrats" focus on personal wealth and military conquest. (Democracy was for him a low form of government, because of people's "undisciplined desires"...)

Fault 64:
Cancer and Terrorism?

Cancer and terrorism are twin scourges of modern humanity, each with Level -2 and -3 properties.

They share further characteristics. Both flourish in different kinds of "cell!" – cancer cells exist in all of us, and the instinct that draws together those who are or feel repressed, mobilizing them towards violent action, may also be more prevalent than we tend to realize. (Those *labeled* terrorists are not alone in terrorizing and killing innocent people, and some later become accepted, even lauded, by former enemies!)

A great deal is known about the *environments* in which both bodily cancer and international terrorism respectively thrive. Much is also known about how to prevent and how to treat both effectively. Yet this knowledge is not fully shared or applied. There are powerful (-2) groups whose interests would not be served by such prevention or healing.

It is said that in ancient China, doctors were paid – and would only agree to receive money – while their patients were *in good health!* Today we are very far from such an ethos and the incentives it would bring.

Fix 64:
Transparency!

Corruption is a term used by people with mindsets +1 and +2 when they observe abusive practices of people with mindsets -1 and -2.

While the most common usage is with reference to the abuse of public funds for personal benefit, we can apply the term more widely to our uses and abuses of our own Mindset and Intelligence and their impact within Society, Citizenship, Education and Government.

Levels of corruption correspond directly to negative levels of Mindset. It's well documented that the flourishing of repressive regimes in Africa, the Middle East and Latin America has been and remains advantageous to powerful interests in the "developed" world. Unless and until such mindsets reform, both cancer and terrorism will surely persist.

The possibility of such reform emanating from the United Nations is a long way off, as its most powerful member states continue to flout what they have signed up to. Thus the UN remains a Level +1 aspirational organization.

It seems our hopes must lie in increasing transparency and in the eventual re-awakening of *conscience*.

Fault 65:
Dependence or Independence?

From an early age, we are aware of the powerful duality of dependence and independence, as we move from relying on parental or other help for food and shelter to become "self-sufficient." Later, others may be dependent upon us in various ways.

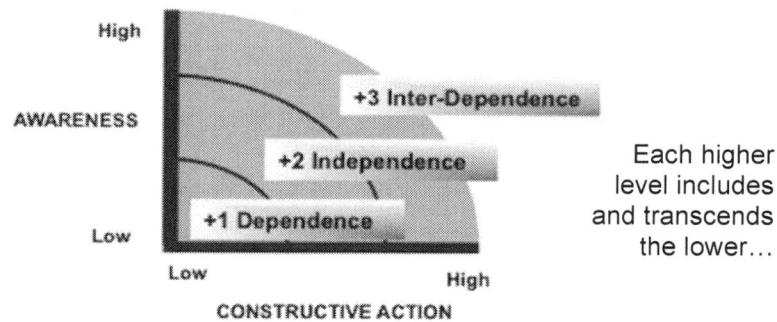

The shift from *independence to inter-dependence*, like other examples of moving from +2 to +3, is less automatic and requires a different kind of effort and energy.

In moving from dependence to independence, the potential gains are clearer; in moving from independence to inter-dependence the potential gains can be less visible than the pain and discomfort of sacrificing *hard-won independence!*

154

Fix 65:
Inter-Dependence!

The relatively *conscious* shift to *constructive inter-dependence* between family members, organizations or nations requires an understanding of the potential benefits of becoming *part* of something bigger. And through the process, the older relationships are transformed.

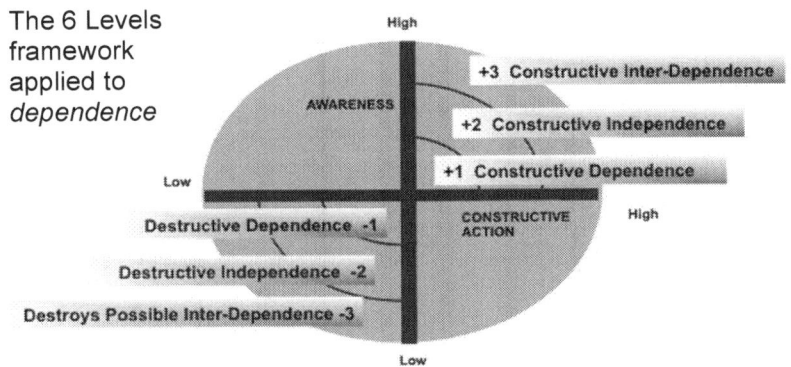

The 6 Levels framework applied to *dependence*

Suggestion: to explore further these different levels and qualities of dependence, try to find examples of *sovereign states* that fit each category shown in the diagram. How is inter-dependence *created?* How do the *destructive* levels develop and what forms do they take? In each case, how do those in power explain the situation and their intentions? What form does *education* take in each?

Fault 66:
Science or Religion?

For several hundred years, the West has struggled with the dichotomy of science and religion both in its attempts to interpret the world and in its political approaches to the exercise of power. In recent decades, this dichotomy has expanded so that we speak of the *knowledge of the West* and the *wisdom of the East.*

Let's recognize these are *not opposites!* Science is primarily a product of *intellectual* intelligence, thriving on the rational-empirical albeit with occasional *intuitive* (+3 EQ) insights. And while there can be both intellectual and physical aspects too, the focus of religion is primarily on raising *emotional* intelligence through the use of stories and analogies. Left brain and right brain, as some put it.

In both religion (which means *re-connecting*) and myths, we should remember the age-old habit of *personifying* what today we might call *energies.* How interesting that the word *myth*, for centuries a vehicle of psychological truth, is currently used to mean *falsehood!*

Wisdom begins with better understanding the present and, as far as we can, how it derived from the past. And then acknowledging that, however much we would like something to be different, right now it's the *only* way it *can* be! Such acknowledgement can start the process…

Fix 66:
Recognize *Decay!*

Applying the 6 Levels framework to *spirituality* and religion, we can quickly see that the 5 "great" religions (the three Abrahamic religions of Judaism, Christianity and Islam, plus Hinduism and Buddhism), have in varying degrees *fallen* from their high origins to include even the *opposite* of the authentic teachings.

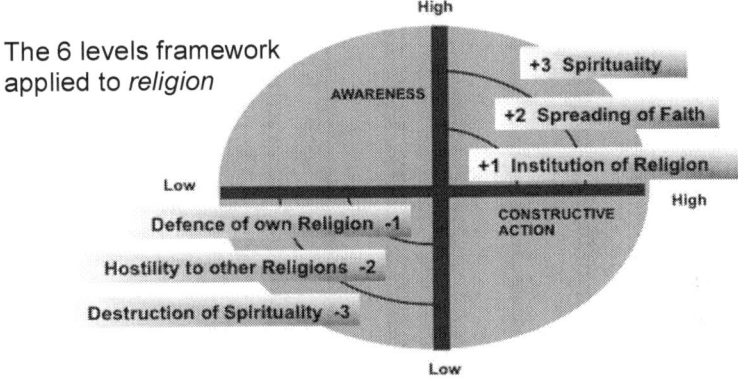

Those claiming to act in the name of such religions may have their center of gravity at any one of the six levels.

What can go unnoticed is the *commonality* of the original messages, adapted to different eras and geographies. An example is the story of Cain slaying his brother Abel, which features in the texts of all 3 Abrahamic religions – and is so relevant today!

Fault 67:
Crime and Punishment?

The reactions of a society to the breaking of its laws vary from protection of the public to vengeance against the perpetrator. As the judge in Gilbert and Sullivan's *Trial by Jury* sings: "My object all sublime, Which I will achieve in time, Is to make the punishment fit the crime, The punishment fit the crime!"

This philosophy of "Eye for an eye, Tooth for a tooth," pervades much of our thinking, so that if the crime is committed with a -2 mindset, the treatment comes from the same level (or lower!).

As has often been observed: "Justice is the interests of the stronger." We conveniently overlook the objectively criminal activity (wars, colonialism, slavery, bullying in all its forms) that helps establish such "strength."

A legal case in 2016 involved a convicted mass murderer winning a lawsuit against government for maltreatment in prison. Among those witnessing the proceedings and even involved in deciding the outcome were friends and relatives of the murderer's victims.

Perhaps this kind of heart-wrenching anguish is indicative of the large-scale process of remorse that humanity must experience if it is to learn and progress.

"Let whoever is free of mistakes cast the first stone."

Fix 67:
Repair and *Prepare!*

Combining and expanding elements from the diagrams in FF60 and FF62, we can picture the types of change needed for repairing a criminal mindset; a movement from relatively low to relatively high awareness and attitude, and a (measureable) shift in the constructiveness of action.

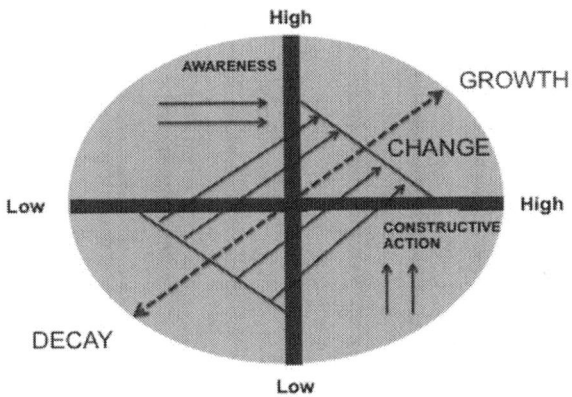

The need to generate a shift from -2 to +2 Mindsets is a species-wide need. Broad approaches are outlined in this book, particularly within FF 11-30.

If we start to visualize the situation of criminals as representative of our collective situation, we will likely be closer to the truth than if we see them as exceptions.

Let's repair the past and *prepare the future!*

Fault 68:
Free Speech or "Correctness"?

The ideal of "free" expression is hampered by the reality of imprisoned, gullible or lazy mindsets. Actually we are all very limited in what we can express!

When we think and speak from Level -1 and -2 mindsets that include negative emotions, arguments and prejudices, we cannot fail to upset others since they equally have their own prejudices and "requirements" of which we (and they!) may or may not be aware.

So should we aim to speak only in positive, constructive terms? This would surely be ideal; at the same time, to *impose* it would be to block the natural and lasting process of development that involves a) *intentionally* deciding and working to avoid expressing negativity, b) *intentionally* channeling negative energy elsewhere, and c) through making a) and b) into habits, gradually *eliminating the formation* of negative thoughts and emotions.

And while some written constitutions promote free speech as long as it does not threaten public order, to impose particular words that must or must not be used connects to the Orwellian nightmare and raises questions once again about the role of government.

"Political correctness" therefore naturally creates its own negative reactions!

Fix 68:
Build *Attentiveness!*

We tend to judge ourselves by our intentions and others by their actions. Others do the same.

And, more subtly, we may very easily, without realizing we are doing it, *project* intentions onto others – the intentions that we subconsciously feel we would have to have in order to do what they are doing!

In communicating to reduce the potentially destructive influence of unseen prejudices, we therefore need to be *attentive* to:

- *Preparing* what we say so that it becomes intentional, not reactive
- Communicating *intent*, so that people don't assume or guess what the intention is
- *Mentally clarifying* what we want to achieve through our words, and checking whether this is the best way to achieve it

Suggestion: if these are new habits that seem interesting to develop, they may be easiest to apply first in emails or other written communication, where there is more time to check negativity and its impact. (Skilled communicators incorporate them into the spoken word, slowing the speed and allowing silences if helpful…)

Fault 69:
Fed up with "Strategy"?

In organizations in different parts of the world, right now, middle managers are feeling or expressing their frustration with "strategy," "strategic initiatives" and the like. Why?

First, because they are not being exposed to or invited to *participate* in strategy as conveyed in this book. Just as large ships can only turn around very slowly, so managers in large organizations are concerned with very slow rates of change and deal almost exclusively with *tactics* – even then not inventing new tactics but tweaking old ones!

Second, because the so-called strategy does not address or connect to the two things they care most about: *themselves* and *their relationships!* Third, because they likely realize that all or most of the strategies and strategic workshops they have been involved with previously achieved little or no *meaningful* results!

What to do about this? Let's take a simple phrase from the lower right quadrant of the Awareness/Action diagram (see FF61): "Sinners, repent!" – a phrase that many find off-putting because of its apparent accusation.

We saw in FF62 that "sin" derives from the notion of "mistake." "Repent" derives from the Latin "think again." So "sinners, repent!" is an exhortation to those who are making mistakes – to *think differently!*

Fix 69:
Think *Differently!*

Strategic thinking as we have approached it in this book has the meaning of *complete* thinking, in the sense of articulating and connecting all forms of creative/open questions (why? what? how? when? where? and so on) within a specific context or situation.

We have called this *Being Strategic* (see FF33). It does not imply or involve the boredom or frustration described on the page opposite. On the contrary, it describes a way to use IQ, EQ and PQ so that we *awaken ourselves and others* from such states and discover inner and outer relationship and meaningful participation.

This different way of thinking begins by *looking upwards* with a question that has been off the radar for too long:

*What is the **contribution** that is needed!*

We need to ask and explore what and how our IQ, EQ and PQ can *contribute!* We need to be able to express what teams, departments, organizations and governments are *contributing*, and to whom or what! We need to ask what international organizations are contributing, and to whom or what!

Once *contribution* has been reviewed, re-defined, clearly articulated and *agreed*, the rest can be thought through!

Fault 70:
Life or Death?

Once again, this dichotomy is not the whole story. There are *three* possibilities, not two!

Individually and collectively, we are a work in progress, regress or repetition! (See FF61.) These are the choices facing us long-term as a species and on a daily basis as leaders and citizens.

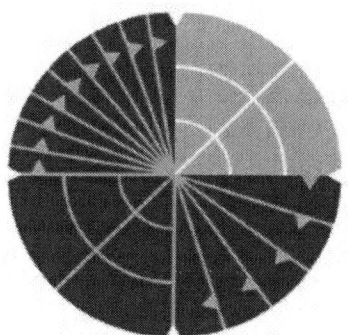

Progress means *growth* – not physical expansion but the balanced and incremental **growth of awareness and constructive action** (see FF57). To generate this growth in oneself and others is the **responsibility of a leader**. There are **9 contexts of leadership**, ranging from Mindset and Intelligence to Organizations and Government.

Fix 70:
Press the *Refresh Button!*

To clarify what this growth signifies in the 9 different contexts, we can identify, test out and gradually understand and apply **6 Levels of relative Awareness and Action** (see FF2).

These Levels apply in *all Leadership Contexts*, and the framework can also be used as an EQ-based analytical tool for many additional contexts and topics – for examples see FF 63, 65 and 66.

An *overview* of how the 6 Levels apply in each of the 9 Contexts is shown in FF57. An *example* of how the different contexts can be tailored, brought together and measured is shown in FF58.

This approach to measurement is designed not for its own sake but to *set direction* for the renewal of growth in each context. For this, it has to be connected to *complete* thinking – the approach to strategic thought set out in FF 12-14.

So *how to press the refresh button?*

Use FF 1-10 to tune up your mindset, then pick a context within which to self-assess (FF 51-60) and create a new, meaningful way forward!

INDEX

58829409R00098

Made in the USA
Charleston, SC
22 July 2016